FIRST CLASS CARGO

A HISTORY OF COMBINATION CARGO-PASSENGER SHIPS

WILLIAM H. MILLER

The History Press

A classic combination passenger-cargo liner, Cunard's 13,500grt *Parthia*, being serviced by a floating grain elevator at New York's Pier 92 in 1953. The far larger 2,233-passenger *Queen Elizabeth* is to the right of the more moderate, 250-passenger *Parthia*. (Port Authority of New York & New Jersey)

First published 2016

The History Press
The Mill, Brimscombe Port
Stroud, Gloucestershire, GL5 2QG
www.thehistorypress.co.uk

British Library Cataloguing in Publication Data.
A catalogue record for this book is available from the British Library.

ISBN 978 0 7509 6508 8

Typesetting and origination by The History Press
Printed in China

Front Cover: The Holland–America combo liners *Dinteldyk* (left) and *Diemerdyk* (right) in a painting by Stephen Card.

Back Cover: The Furness combo liner *Newfoundland* in a painting by Stephen Card. (Alan Davidson)

CONTENTS

ACKNOWLEDGEMENTS

Much like operating the ships in these pages, preparing a book requires many hands. Like the captain on the bridge, I rely heavily on my crew – the many contributors to this book. First, I must thank The History Press and especially Amy Rigg for taking on this particular title. It is slightly different from our usual work with the big liners.

Special thanks to Stephen Card, a great artist, for the use of his splendid paintings as cover material, both here and in many other of my books. Other special contributors include Richard Faber, Norman Knebel, Captain James McNamara and Albert Wilhelmi, as well as the late Andrew Kilk, whose generosity was much appreciated. Added special thanks to Anthony La Forgia and, for technical assistance, Michael Hadgis. Special appreciation also to Tom Jones for his insightful foreword.

Other 'hands on deck' deserving of my appreciation include: Ernest Arroyo, Philippe Brebant, Alice Carrender, Luis Miguel Correia, the late Frank Cronican, the late Julio Del Valle, the late Alex Duncan, Peter Edwards, the late John Gillespie, Robert Gordon, Robert Hughes, John Jones, Dr David Kirkman, Michael D.J. Lennon, G. Monteny, John Morgan, Hisashi Noma, Richard Remnant, Captain Klaus Schacht, Captain Heinz-Dieter Schmidt, Roger Sherlock, Steffen Weirauch and the late Joseph Wilhelm.

Companies and other organisations that provided assistance include the Bibby Line, Blue Star Line, Booth Line, China Navigation Company, Compagnie Maritime Belge, Eastern & Australian Line, Ellerman Lines, Grace Line, Halifax Maritime Museum, Hapag-Lloyd, Hamburg–South America Line, Ivaran Lines, MOPASS, M&W Towing & Transportation Company, New Zealand Shipping Company, Orient Overseas Line, P&O, Port Authority of New York & New Jersey, Royal Rotterdam Lloyd, South China Morning Post Ltd, Steamship Historical Society of America, World Ocean & Cruise Liner Society and the World Ship Society.

Anyone overlooked in error or haste has my advance apology.

FOREWORD

Like the author, Bill Miller, I too liked combo ships, those great blends of a passenger ship and a freighter. They were a very unique sort of ship and I was fortunate to have sailed as a steward on several of them: the *Worcestershire*, *Argentina Star*, *Ceramic* and *Ruahine*. They were all British-owned, of course, and very viable ships still in the 1950s, with many features in common, especially in the passenger quarters with lots of woodwork, lino floors and public bathroom facilities. They were intimate, inviting, almost like big yachts. Service, especially in the dining rooms, was more select, more personalised and certainly moved at a slower pace than, say, first class in the *Queen Mary*. We would have some very interesting passengers aboard as well, including top government officials, colonial administrators, wealthy tourists and even minor royalty. It was well known, for example, that Princess Alice, a great aunt to the queen, liked travelling out to the Caribbean on the Fyffes Line ships and to Australia on Blue Funnel. On a 50–100-passenger ship, however, she was just one of the guests.

Formal but informal as well, that was a combo ship. I was very fortunate to have sailed and served in some of them. They are almost all gone now, but what a great age in shipping they belonged to! In his book, Bill Miller has given me and his many readers a nostalgic review.

Tom Jones
Liverpool, England

INTRODUCTION

I've always thought combination passenger-cargo ships were very interesting – the select balance of considerable cargo being carried along with passengers and usually in very high-standard accommodations. In New York Harbor, where I began watching ships in the 1950s, especially the great liners, there were many combo liners about. I remember seeing the likes of the *President Monroe*, *Exeter*, *Rio de la Plata*, *Israel*, *Noordam*, *Santa Sofia* and *Ancon*. These ships featured in the daily passenger ship schedules of the *New York Times* and the *Herald Tribune*. They were different to ordinary freighters. They alone adhered to fixed schedules and had specific sailing times. I also saw some of the more exotic combo ships, such as the *African Enterprise*, *Hrvatska* and *Monte Urquiola*. They were all fascinating ships, even curious in ways, and those wonderfully insightful passenger ship books by the likes of Laurence Dunn added to the story of the combo liners.

In later years, there were added treats, such as the World Ship Society's Port of New York Branch meeting aboard the innovative *Savannah*, a tour of the laid-up *Exochorda* and a walk around the *Cristóbal*, which had recently been downgraded to a freighter. In 1992, I sailed from Rio de Janeiro northward to New York aboard the luxurious *Americana*. Although she had a capacity for up to eighty-eight passengers, there were just twenty-four on board that voyage. It was my chance to experience a ship that was not quite a liner or cruise ship, but much more than a freighter with twelve passenger berths. It was very comfortable and very relaxing, but with none of the ambience and tone of, say, a big passenger ship. I recall, among other remembrances, everyone seemed to nap from 2 p.m. until 4 p.m. each day. In the passenger areas, the *Americana* was dead quiet.

Because of the limitations of this book, I confess that not all the combo liners are included. China had many of them, for example, all built in more recent years, while other combo ships simply do not get extensive treatment. They have been sufficiently covered, I felt, in other, earlier books, including titles by me. Nevertheless, I wanted to do a sort of review of those wonderful but now largely bygone combo liners.

Bill Miller
Secaucus, New Jersey, USA

ALCOA STEAMSHIP COMPANY

*ALCOA CAVALIER, ALCOA CLIPPER
AND ALCOA CORSAIR*

Amidst the extensive ship model collection at New York's South Street Seaport, there is a fine waterline model of these Alcoa passenger-cargo liners. They were great examples of a very basic cargo ship, a standardised wartime Victory ship, redesigned and made over as first-class passenger-carrying ships. The 8,481grt trio *Alcoa Cavalier*, *Aloca Clipper* and *Alcoa Corsair* sailed on a three-week rotation: New Orleans to Caribbean ports and then return to Mobile. They were fully air-conditioned, had private bathrooms in every room (for the ninety-five maximum passengers) and an outdoor pool.

AMERICAN EXPORT LINES

EXCALIBUR, EXCAMBION, EXETER AND EXOCHORDA

These ships were regulars to the New Jersey side of the Hudson River at New York. Until 1956 they berthed at Pier D in Jersey City, after which they used Pier B of the newly renovated Hoboken Port Authority piers. These fine-looking ships with their cigar-shaped funnels were quite unique and they almost always berthed bow-out rather than stern-out. The American Export marine superintendent, it was said, preferred it that way. It made for an easier, quicker departure.

When, after the dark days of the Second World War, the New York-based American Export Lines looked to re-establish its transatlantic passenger

The handsome *Alcoa Corsair* and her two sisters were painted largely in silver – reminders of the aluminium produced by their owners, Alcoa, the Aluminium Company of America. (James McNamara Collection)

Outbound for the Mediterranean on a Friday at 4 p.m., the *Excambion* has departed from Jersey City and passes the Lower Manhattan skyline. (James McNamara Collection)

service to and from the Mediterranean it had a bit of a struggle. Its 1931-built quartet, the 125-passenger *Excalibur*, *Excambion*, *Exeter* and *Exochorda*, were all gone, casualties of battle or, in the case of the *Exochorda*, sold off to Turkey to become the national flagship *Tarsus*. From their offices at 39 Broadway in Lower Manhattan's busy shipping district, American Export directors were forced to look to some wartime-built transports that might be converted in a post-war era to so-called 'combo ships', a practical blend of combination passenger-cargo liners. Four ships were acquired from the US government and, after rebuilding, hoisted American Export colours in 1948. They became the 'new' *Excalibur*, *Excambion*, *Exeter* and *Exochorda*.

Measuring 9,600 tons and 473ft in length, they were superbly refitted for only 125 all-first-class passengers. The remaining revenue would come from five holds of freight. Their accommodations were in fact newsworthy, as they were among the very finest at sea at the time. Coupled with a

On the afternoon of 27 June 1950, the outbound *Excalibur* detoured too closely to the Brooklyn skyline in Lower New York Bay and collided with the Danish freighter *Colombia*, which caught fire. Both ships were badly damaged. (Cronican-Arroyo Collection)

series of modern public rooms, ample deck space and an outdoor pool, every stateroom was fitted with a private bathroom. But more importantly for the late 1940s, they were fully air-conditioned – in fact, the very first completely 'cooled' passenger ships yet to sail. Soon, American Export would incorporate this cherished amenity into its mightiest ships, the *Independence* and *Constitution* of 1950–51.

The 'Four Aces' sailed every other Friday from their owner's Jersey City (and later Hoboken) terminal. They ran a six-week service that covered the complete length of the Mediterranean. Passengers could sail between ports, make Atlantic crossings or take the voyage as a full forty-four-day cruise. By the late 1950s, minimum fares for such a cruise started at $960 or $19 a day! Although their actual itineraries were often changed, the final schedule of ports read: New York across to Cádiz, Barcelona, Marseilles, Naples, Alexandria, Beirut, Naples, Marseilles, Genoa, Livorno, Barcelona and then homewards to Boston and finally New York.

But quite regrettably, especially in view of the rather harsh economics of running very costly US-flag passenger ships, this quartet had only about ten years of profitable service. Two of them, the *Excambion* and *Exochorda*, were withdrawn in 1958–59. After being 'mothballed' for a time, they found other lives not with passengers but in education: the *Excambion* became the Texas A&M University training ship *Texas Clipper*; the *Exochorda* went to Stevens Institute of Technology of Hoboken for use as a floating dormitory, the *Stevens*, until broken up at nearby Kearny and then Jersey City in 1979. The *Texas Clipper*, actually the last survivor, was laid up for some years before being sunk as a reef off Texas in June 2007.

The *Exeter* and *Excalibur* steamed on until 1964, when they too were retired from American Export service and then went on to other lives. Hoisting the colours of the Orient Overseas Line, owned by Taiwanese shipping tycoon C.Y. Tung (he would later buy Cunard's *Queen Elizabeth* as well as the *Independence* and *Constitution*), they became the *Oriental Pearl* and

Beginning in 1967 and until 1975, the former *Exochorda* – renamed *Stevens* – spent time as a floating dormitory at Stevens Institute of Technology in Hoboken, New Jersey. (James McNamara Collection)

Oriental Jade respectively. Chinese artworks were brought aboard to enhance their essentially American décor of stainless steel, vinyl and glossy linoleums. The pair sailed on sixty-day Far East cruises from San Francisco. A great bargain even then, the full voyages started at $880 or just $15 a day!

The former *Exeter* and *Excalibur* sailed for nearly ten years, until 1974, when age coupled with an enormous increase in worldwide fuel oil prices sent them off to Taiwanese scrapyards.

SAVANNAH

The 13,600grt was perhaps the most unique of all combo liners – she was nuclear-powered. Launched in July 1959, the 595ft-long ship, with high-standard accommodations for up to sixty passengers, entered commercial service in 1962. Used on various routes including New York–Mediterranean ports and at first operated by the States Marine Lines but mostly by American Export Lines, she was a grand bid to display nuclear power being used for peaceful purposes. She was not an economic success, however, and was soon downgraded to all-freighter status and, in less than ten years, laid up. Later

The futuristic *Savannah* is seen at Barcelona with the liner *Independence* berthed across the harbour. Both ships were operated by American Export Lines. (James McNamara Collection)

used as a museum ship at Savannah, Georgia, and then Charleston, South Carolina, she was placed in the US government Reserve Fleet near Norfolk, Virginia, in 1994. Later she was moved to Baltimore with the intention of remaking her as a museum ship.

AMERICAN PRESIDENT LINES

PRESIDENT MONROE AND *PRESIDENT POLK*

Very often, I would one see of this pair in New York Harbor at Pier 9, Jersey City. Busily, they might be canted over, leaning to one side as the cargo was being offloaded. Freight barges would be along the outer side of the ship and sometimes a big, heavy-lift floating crane (owned in those times by Merrit, Chapman & Scott) might be there as well, handling some large piece of cargo. The *President Monroe* and *President Polk* tended to arrive at New York, offload and then sail off on a ten- to twelve-day 'coastal swing' – to Boston, Philadelphia, Baltimore and Norfolk to collect additional cargo – and then return to New York or Jersey City for a final loading and the boarding of passengers before heading on a 100-day itinerary around the world.

In those days, American President Lines ran three services from New York and other US east coast ports: around the world, the Far East and inter-coastal to California. In the 1950s and '60s, in those final eras before the massive shift to containerised cargo shipping, APL berths in New York Harbor were rarely empty. Their ships had presidential names – *President McKinley*, *President Adams* and *President Fillmore*. But of special note to me were a pair of identical sister ships – the *President Monroe* and *President Polk*. Because they carried as many as ninety-six passengers each and more than the usual twelve berths of the company freighters, their comings and goings were noted in the daily passenger ship schedules of the *New York Times* and the long-gone *New York Herald Tribune*. Unlike the freighters, both ships had much more of a fixed schedule.

Originally built in 1940 at the famed Newport News Shipyards in Virginia, there were to be as many as seven sister ships. But after very strenuous work in the Second World War, only two of them, the *Monroe* and the *Polk*, were returned to American President commercial service. (Three larger, more luxurious ships, the 125-passenger *President Jackson*, *President Hayes* and *President Adams*, were to have been added in the early 1950s, but then were taken over while still under construction by the US government for much needed duty in the Korean War.) The *Monroe* and *Polk* were very popular

A 5 p.m. sailing: the *President Monroe* departs from Jersey City's Pier 9 on another around-the-world voyage. (Moran Towing & Transportation Company)

ships. They were noted for their crisp service and fine cuisine, the smartness of their passenger quarters (which included the novelty of a fireplace in the main lounge), the amenity of an outdoor pool and sun deck, and the fact that every cabin had a private bathroom – still a noted distinction in late 1940s and '50s ocean travel. Their only infirmity seems to have been their lack of complete air conditioning. (Actually, the restaurant, bar, lounge and a few cabins were air-conditioned, but the system did not cover the entire ship – foyers, corridors and some staterooms.) While open portholes at sea had their advantages as well as a sense of romance about them, such areas on these ships could be floating infernos while sitting in ports in India and in summertime Japan and Italy.

The round trips of these two President combo ships were scheduled well over a year in advance, but could also be broken into port-to-port segments. The routing from Pier 9, Jersey City was to Cristobal, Balboa, Acapulco, San Francisco, Honolulu, Yokohama, Kobe, Hong Kong, Saigon, Singapore, Penang, Cochin, Bombay, Karachi, Suez, Port Said, Alexandria, Naples, Marseilles, Genoa, Leghorn and finally back home. In 1963, fares for the full 100 days started at $2,900 (or $30 per person per day). Actually, like most American-flag passenger ships, they were comparatively expensive. Minimum fare for the then new *Rotterdam's* eighty-day world cruise was

$2,700, while a ninety-day trip on another Dutch liner, the *Willem Ruys*, out of Port Everglades, Florida, was $1,350 in first class and a bargain $840 in tourist class (or just $10 per person per day!).

Inevitably, the 9,500-ton *President Monroe* and *President Polk* fell out of step with increasingly sophisticated, more accountant-ruled passenger shipping. They were replaced with ultra-luxurious cargo liners, but which had limited quarters, for only a dozen passengers, and therefore no need for extra stewards and entertainments or even a doctor. In 1965 the *Monroe* was sold to the Greek tanker tycoon John S. Latsis, who used the ship only part-time, to carry Muslim religious pilgrims to Jeddah in Saudi Arabia. She was renamed *Marianna VI*, but sailed for only a few years, until 1969, when she went to Hong Kong wreckers. The *Polk* went to an unknown Liberian-flag company and became the *Gaucho Martin Fierro*, a 'cattle boat' used in the Argentine meat trades. Later renamed *Minotaurus*, she went out east in 1970 and was scrapped on Taiwan.

A decade or so later, in the early 1980s, American President Lines would end all passenger services on its freighters and instead concentrate on the ever-expanding, ever-competitive age of bigger and bigger container ships. A pity in many ways that this push-button, highly computerised, dollar-watching age has eclipsed that earlier, more charismatic and certainly more romantic era of such ships as the *President Monroe* and *President Polk*.

ARGENTINE STATE LINE

RIO DE LA PLATA, *RIO JACHAL* AND *RIO TUNUYAN*

I well remember this trio of liners from their times along the lower New York City waterfront. They berthed at Pier 25, at the foot of Franklin Street in the City's Tribeca district. By the late 1950s and as combination passenger-cargo ships, they had rather typical long stays in port – arriving on Saturday mornings and remaining alongside for six days, until sailing at 5 o'clock on Friday. Pier 25 was not especially tall, and so these ships – with their blue funnels and white superstructures – stood out. Operated by the Buenos Aires-based Argentine State Line, they were represented at New York by one of the port's more prominent agents: Boyd, Weir & Sewell Inc.

These three handsome ships were created especially for service to North America and, in some ways, to compete with the long-established, US-flag Moore McCormack Lines' trio of *Argentina*, *Brazil* and *Uruguay*. This new

The late-afternoon maiden arrival of the *Rio Jachal* in the lower Hudson River. (Cronican-Arroyo Collection)

The bedroom of a suite aboard the *Rio Tunuyan*. (Author's Collection)

trio was in fact modified versions of the Dodero Line threesome: *Argentina*, *Uruguay* and *Libertad*, which had been built in England. Slightly larger, with 116 first-class berths only, they came from Italian shipbuilders the Ansaldo yards at Genoa. The 550ft-long *Rio de la Plata* was commissioned first, in April 1950, the *Rio Jachal* in the following September and the *Rio Tunuyan* in April 1951. A year later, following the death of the hugely popular Eva Péron, the *Rio Tunuyan* was renamed *Evita*, a name she carried until the regime of Juan Péron was toppled and ousted in 1955. She then reverted to her original name.

Their general routing was similar to the three combo liners on the run to London. There was a sailing from New York every other Friday, bound for

Trinidad or La Guaira, Rio de Janeiro, Santos, Montevideo and Buenos Aires. In the early 1960s, these ships also offered forty-three-day round-trip cruises with fares beginning at $1,080 or approximately $25 per person per day. Advertising referred to the 'Route of the Rio liners'.

The accommodation was arranged on five decks and the public rooms consisted of a forward lounge, a full cinema, library, writing room, smoking room, main dining room and a special children's dining room. On deck there was a swimming pool as well as a games area. The cabins, all of which were air-conditioned, had either private or semi-private bathroom facilities.

Within a decade, by the early 1960s, the requirements for passenger-cargo liners on the South American run to and from New York began to decline – and quickly. Consequently, plans were made to rebuild both the *Rio de la Plata* and *Rio Tunuyan* with increased capacities and for an all-tourist-class service to Hamburg. At the same time, in 1962, the Argentine State Line (Flota Mercante del Estado) was merged with the Ultramar Line (the former Dodero Line) to together form the ELMA Lines.

Soon afterwards, on 28 September 1962, the long, sad saga of the third sister, the *Rio Jachal*, began. She suffered a night-time fire at Pier 25 in New York. She was badly damaged, her upper works scorched. The 12-year-old ship was soon taken to the Todd Shipyards, located in the Eire Basin in nearby Brooklyn for inspection, examination and some repairs before returning to Argentina. Instead, however, she was moved to the pier on 27th Street, also in Brooklyn, and remained there for well over a year. In April 1964, under the care of a reduced crew, she finally sailed to Buenos Aires, presumably for full repairs but was then laid up again. Four years later, on 17 April 1968, she caught fire once more and this time was destroyed beyond all economic repair. A year later, she was towed to local ship breakers at Buenos Aires and then waited another year before being demolished in 1970.

In 1963, the *Rio de la Plata* was refitted with increased accommodations for 372 all-tourist-class passengers. Her new career on the run to northern Europe was very brief, however. Late in the following year, on 19 November, while lying at a shipyard berth in Buenos Aires harbour, she caught fire and burnt out completely. Her wreckage was finally scrapped, however, four years later, in 1968.

The *Rio Tunuyan* survived the longest and, following her 1963–64 refit (with extended quarters for 372 all-tourist-class passengers), was assigned to the Buenos Aires–Hamburg run with the equally enlarged *Libertad*. Several years later, as this north European service began its decline, she was teamed with France's *Pasteur*, but only on a seasonal schedule. In the northern summer season, from May to November, she made regular crossings. For the remainder of the year she was used for cruising from Buenos Aires to the Straits of Magellan, the Antarctic and along the Brazilian coast. Following her final cruises, she was retired on 30 January 1972 and laid up. She was broken up for scrap five years later, in the spring of 1977, at San Pedro, Argentina.

BIBBY LINE

WORCESTERSHIRE, DERBYSHIRE, WARWICKSHIRE AND *LEICESTERSHIRE*

When still in my student days in the early 1960s, I began a letter-writing campaign to steamship lines all over the world. I was writing to request brochures, deck plans, sailing schedules and, most especially, either postcards or photographs. Included on my list was the Bibby Line, then located in Liverpool. They were quick to reply, in a precise letter on onion-skin paper, announcing that in 1964 they were discontinuing their passenger services altogether and instead running twelve-passenger freighters only, and included a brochure. I shall always remember the closing of that letter: 'Your kind and humble servant, the Bibby Line Limited'.

Believe it or not, Bibby is still in business! While almost all of the great British shipping lines are gone (with the obvious exception of Cunard and P&O, which are owned by Miami-based Carnival Corporation), the Bibby Line – dating from as far back as 1807 – lives on. Based in Liverpool, they still have shipping interests as well as a floating hotel (they even owned floating dorms for soldiers), foodstuff and financial services. Up until 1964, Bibby operated passenger-cargo ships on the long-distance run out to Burma (now Myanmar). The general routing was from Liverpool to Gibraltar, Marseilles, Port Said, the Suez Canal, Port Sudan, Colombo and finally to Rangoon. Sturdy, sort of no-nonsense ships with few frills and with names like *Warwickshire*, *Leicestershire* and *Worcestershire*, they carried 75–125 passengers in simple but comfortable quarters. Robert Gordon sailed as steward on Bibby ships almost until the last voyages in the early 1960s. We met recently over breakfast:

We had government and business people mostly and sometimes with their entire families, but we also sold the long trips out to Rangoon and back as a sort of cruise … Emphasis was placed on the relaxing, very healthy days at sea. Daily life for the passengers was quite simple. There were, of course, the three

Seen in the River Mersey at Liverpool, the *Warwickshire* was a typically handsome combination passenger-cargo ship with cargo holds fore and aft, and a good-sized midship superstructure. (Gillespie-Faber Collection)

meals and afternoon tea. But after dinner, it might be just egg & spoon races or a quiz or just listening to records. It might seem boring, particularly by today's busy cruise liner standards, but we had passengers that preferred being bored – well, being very comfortably bored.

The *Worcestershire*, dating from 1931, was the oldest in the Bibby fleet by the early 1960s; the *Derbyshire* followed four years later. Originally built for 300 passengers, they were rebuilt following war service with quarters for 115 all-first-class passengers. The *Worcestershire* was retired in 1961 after being sold to Japanese scrappers as the renamed *Kannon Maru*. The *Derbyshire* followed three years later, going to Hong Kong breakers.

The 9,000grt *Warwickshire* and *Leicestershire* were post-war ships, completed in 1948–49 and carrying seventy-six passengers each. The *Leicestershire* took a four-year break when, between 1950 and 1954, she sailed on the London–East Africa run while under charter to the British

India Line. Used in Bibby passenger service until 1964, they served briefly as twelve-passenger freighters before being sold to Greek buyers the Typaldos Lines. Renamed *Hania* and *Heraklion* for Adriatic and Aegean ferry services, the *Hania* was extensively rebuilt and for a time listed as the world's largest ferry, carrying 1,450 passengers, 100 cars and 80 coaches. It was all short-lived for her sister *Heraklion*. Caught in a violent Aegean storm on 8 December 1966, she capsized and sank within fifteen minutes. There were a headline-making 241 casualties. In the Greek government inquiry that followed, she was found to be unsafely loaded. As a result, Typaldos and its entire fleet were seized and the owners sent to prison. The *Hania* (ex-*Warwickshire*) was laid up, but then auctioned off in 1971 to the Kavounides Line, only to be resold a year later to Hellenic Cruises, who renamed her *Sirius*. She was not used, however, and sat idle for eight years before being fully scrapped.

The thirty-passenger *Perseus* passing through the Straits of Gibraltar, bound for the Far East. (Gillespie-Faber Collection)

An evocative sketch of the *Leicestershire*. Although a sister to the *Warwickshire*, this 8,922grt vessel was not given an aft mast. (Bibby Line)

The intimate bar and lounge aboard the *Leicestershire*. (Bibby Line)

BLUE FUNNEL LINE

HELENUS, JASON, HECTOR, IXION, PELEUS, PYRRHUS, PATROCLUS AND *PERSEUS*

Once one of Britain's biggest and most successful shipowners, Liverpool-based Blue Funnel's ships mostly looked very similar, all of them capped by distinctive blue and black funnels. The company had a vast freighter fleet, over fifty ships in all in the mid 1950s, some carrying up to a dozen passengers. There were two sets of exceptions: the quartet of the so-called P Class – *Peleus, Pyrrhus, Patroclus* and *Perseus* – for the UK–Austrailia service; and the four sisters of the slightly modified H Class – *Helenus, Jason, Hector* and *Ixion* – for the UK–Far East run.

John Morgan worked back in the 1960s for Britain's Blue Funnel Line. He was assigned to *Ixion*, a sturdy passenger-cargo liner that carried nearly three dozen all-first-class passengers (using some added cots) on the long-haul run from Liverpool out to the Far East, to Singapore, Hong Kong, Kobe and Yokohama. He also served aboard the same company's *Pyrrhus*, which was on the Australian run out of Liverpool to Fremantle, Melbourne and Sydney:

I was a bathroom steward and my daily duties included scheduling the passenger bathing, running a tub and then cleaning it afterward. There were very few private bathrooms attached to cabins in those days and instead passengers used public facilities located along the corridor. Little rooms with polished wood doors contained bathtubs. My duties also included supplying a fresh towel. Even with as few as thirty passengers, it really wasn't very difficult. Some passengers bathed only every other day or even every third day back then.

C.M. Squarey gave them a good appraisal, writing, 'The cabins are notably spacious and even down to the smallest fitting are very thoughtfully planned. The collapsible "morning tea" bedside table is a pleasant novelty.'

The *Pyrrhus* was badly damaged by fire while berthed in the Liverpool docks on 12 November 1964. The event was a prelude – a year later all of these ships were downgraded to twelve-passenger freighter status. Their passenger trade was declining. All eight sisters were sold off to scrap merchants in Taiwan in 1972.

The quarters aboard these Blue Funnel combo ships were very comfortable, immaculately maintained and very British. (Andrew Kilk Collection)

CENTAUR

The name *Centaur* was to the port of Singapore, one of the world's busiest harbours, what the *Queen Mary* was to Southampton, *Nieuw Amsterdam* to Rotterdam or *Lurline* to San Francisco. In 1984, after nearly decades of Singapore–Fremantle service and then a year's charter to South Africa, the *Centaur* was laid up and out of work. She was anchored for some time off Sentosa Island, awaiting her fate. In July 1984 I had the chance to visit the last true Blue Funnel Line passenger ship.

When the 7,990grt *Centaur* was under construction in 1963 at Scotland's John Brown Shipyard, her owner was still one of the world's mightiest shipowners. Blue Funnel ships were well known. Its ships were traditionally beautiful and superbly proportioned, used names derived from Greek mythology and had some of the most distinctive funnels at sea, each painted in vivid blue with a black top. The Liverpool-based company had deep interests in the Middle and Far East, and Singapore might well have been considered a second home. The 480ft-long *Centaur* was built for the firm's last passenger run, replacing two little pre-war running mates, the *Charon* and *Gorgon*.

Commissioned in January 1964, the *Centaur* stopped at Liverpool and then sailed to the east, briefly served as an Australian trade fair ship in Far Eastern waters and then took up her duties on the run to and from Fremantle. She could take 190 all-first-class passengers (206 was the absolute maximum), who were accommodated on three principal decks: Promenade, Bridge and Shelter. An outdoor pool, partially covered by a canvas awning, was fitted aft on the Promenade Deck, and the surrounding lido area was used occasionally as an open-air night-time cinema. Also located on the Promenade Deck was the library (also used for afternoon taped music concerts, church services, etc.) and two suites, each with a bedroom, sitting room and full bath. A bar-lounge, gift shop and ten other cabins filled out this deck. The Bridge Deck included the Governor's Bar (also used as a meeting room), a launderette, hospital and thirty-nine cabins (seventeen of which were without private facilities). A twenty-four-hour self-service 'cuppa tea' pantry proved a popular amenity. On the Shelter Deck, there was a dining room (which was used in the afternoon for children's films), poker machines and thirty-nine additional cabins (only three of which had a private shower and toilet).

The *Centaur* was of rather unique design, as her passenger areas were aft while the cargo was carried forward. Among combination passenger-cargo liners, she was quite unusual in being specially fitted to transport sheep and cattle from Australian ports to Singapore. When she was completely withdrawn from service, in September 1982, the *Centaur* had carried a total of

73,200 passengers, 1.1 million sheep, 17,000 cattle, 1,100 horses and 390,000 tons of general cargo. So popular was she with sea travellers, even near the end of her career, that her owners ran $50 cruises 'to nowhere' out of Singapore. Jeremy Gray, of Blue Funnel in Singapore, added, 'Some 65 per cent of her passengers in the end were loyalist repeaters. Even the Australian dockers, known as "wharfies", exempted her from their frequent strikes.' Dr David Kirkman served as the surgeon aboard the *Centaur* and fondly recalled the ship:

> In her early days, the *Centaur* also sailed to the north-west of western Australia, to load cattle at the ports of Broome and Derby. Specially designed with a flatbottom, there were 20–25ft tidal changes in those ports, and the ship would be left high-and-dry until the next incoming tide. You could walk completely around the 8,000-ton vessel, but then quite suddenly, the inbound tide would come in faster than you could run. Also and quite notably, two governors of western Australia, one of whom was the former master of the Royal Yacht *Britannia*, were installed aboard the *Centaur*. They would sail from Singapore and then take the oath upon arrival at Fremantle. There was such a link to this ship that a western Australian television company made a film about her final sailing from Fremantle. Everyone in western Australia had at least heard of the *Centaur*.

However, by the early 1980s, the *Centaur* was an impractical blend of passenger and cargo ship. The mere 200 passenger berths were simply not enough to pay her way or justify her existence. Concurrently, the sheep trade had gone to a new generation of specialised carriers, while the general freight business shifted to container ships. Even her original owners, Blue Funnel at Liverpool, had shrunk to a mere fraction of their original size. After 303 voyages, the *Centaur* was withdrawn in September 1982.

The *Centaur* had changed from British to local Singapore registry in 1973, when she was transferred to the China Mutual Steam Navigation Company, a division of the Blue Funnel group. However, shortly thereafter her ownership was changed again, this time to Straits Steamship Company of Singapore.

New look: On her maiden voyage in 1963, the engines-aft *Centaur* represented a new design for combination ships. (World Ship Society)

In February 1981, another local shipowner, the Pacific International Lines, became a partner. This ever-changing saga continued when Straits reverted to being full owners and then, in November 1983, was itself bought out by the Keppel Shipyard, which was owned by the government of Singapore. The well-known Blue Funnel name continued, however, but as Blue Funnel Cruises, a division of Straits Steamship Company and operators of the chartered cruise ship *Princess Mahsuri*, the former German-owned *Berlin*.

Prompted by the sudden Falklands War and the extended requisitioning of its little passenger ship *St Helena*, Britain's Curnow Shipping Company chartered the laid-up *Centaur*, beginning in November 1982. Her important but temporary routing was between Avonmouth, Ascension, St Helena and Cape Town. This phase ended in January 1984 when the *St Helena* resumed sailing; the *Centaur* made a nostalgic farewell run with fare-paying passengers aboard from Cape Town to Fremantle and then to Singapore. According to Jeremy Gray, 'This voyage marked the end of an era, the end of a local institution in Singapore.'

Laid up and in the care of six crewmembers, she was offered for sale at $2.5 million, but there were no takers in the beginning. She was in remarkably tidy condition during my visit. The enormous captain's dayroom is used to receive prospective buyers (and curious guests), and there still seems to be some life aboard the otherwise silent *Centaur*. She was finally sold in 1985, becoming the Chinese *Hai Long* and later *Hai Da*. Having sailed mostly from Shanghai, she was finally demolished in China in 1995.

BLUE STAR LINE

ARGENTINA STAR, *BRASIL STAR*, *URUGUAY STAR* AND *PARAGUAY STAR*

Sometimes I'd see Blue Star Line freighters berthed in the vast cargo piers of New Jersey, several miles west of New York at Port Newark. They tended to be large ships, some as much as 550ft in length, but best recalled for their often huge, sometimes almost overpowering funnels. London-based Blue Star had a huge cargo fleet in the 1950s and '60s, in fact the twilight years of the mighty British merchant navy, but the company was headed, it might be said, by a quartet of combination passenger-cargo ships steadily used on the UK–South America route. They were appropriately named, *Argentina Star*, *Brasil Star*, *Uruguay Star* and *Paraguay Star*.

BLUE STAR LINE
accommodation plans

Argentina Star
Brasil Star
Paraguay Star
Uruguay Star

Carrying just over fifty passengers each, the quartet of combo ships operated by London-based Blue Star Line were very popular. (Andrew Kilk Collection)

The wood-panelled lounge aboard the *Brasil Star* provided a charming retreat for days at sea. (Richard Faber Collection)

The *Paraguay Star* was swept by fire while lying in the London Docks in August 1969 and thereafter was sold for scrap. The other three steamed on until 1972 when finally they passed to Taiwanese scrappers.

WINTER VOYAGES
to fabulous
SOUTH AMERICA by
BLUE STAR

THESE are *exclusively first-class* passages which guarantee sun, interest, entertainment, superb accommodation and cuisine, no currency difficulties   for winter weary Britons.

ITINERARY From London via Portugal, Madeira to Buenos Aires calling at Salvador Rio de Janeiro, Santos (Brazil) and Montevideo (Uruguay). Passengers not wishing to stay in Buenos Aires may go ashore at Montevideo and stop in Carrasco or Punta del Este.   NO VISAS are required for Uruguay and Argentina by passengers holding British passports issued in the U.K.

BLUE STAR
LINE ⭐

- **PARAGUAY STAR** Dec. 21
- **IBERIA STAR** Jan. 4
- **BRASIL STAR** Jan. 11
- **ARGENTINA STAR** Jan. 25
- **URUGUAY STAR** Feb. 8

Passenger Office: 3 Lower Regent Street, S.W.1 WHI 2266
Head Office: Albion House, Leadenhall St., E.C.3. ROYal 4567
Branch Offices: Liverpool, Manchester, Birmingham, Glasgow and Bradford.

Winter voyages, escaping the dreary British winter weather, were especially popular on the Blue Star ships to South America. Round-trip voyages were between sixty and seventy days long with most of it in sunshine. (Blue Star Line)

In the late 1950s, the 503ft-long *Brasil Star* and her sisters were made more attractive with a new lavender-grey hull colouring. (Alex Duncan)

IBERIA STAR

In 1963, Blue Star added a fifth passenger-cargo liner, Booth Line's *Anselm*, originally Compagnie Maritime Belge's *Thysville* (built in 1950). Renamed *Iberia Star*, she was rebuilt with seventy-six all-first-class berths for the South American trade. It was very short-lived, however. Within the year, she was transferred to a Blue Star affiliate, the Austasia Line, and became the *Australasia* for Fremantle–Singapore service. She was broken up at Hualien, on Taiwan, in the summer of 1973.

Blue Star Line
IBERIA STAR ACCOMMODATION PLAN

Acquired from the Belgian Line, the slightly larger *Iberia Star* supplemented the original Blue Star quartet on the South American run in the early 1960s. (Andrew Kilk Collection)

A rather sweeping view of the main lounge: This spacious lounge was intended for as few as seventy-six passengers aboard the *Iberia Star*. (Andrew Kilk Collection)

BOOTH LINE

HILDEBRAND AND *HUBERT*

Even in the heyday of traditional passenger ship travel, the services to the exotic and remote River Amazon provided by Britain's Booth Line were quite unique. Their ships were routed between Liverpool via Leixões, Lisbon and Madeira over to Barbados and Trinidad, then Belem and finally 1,000 miles along the Amazon to Manaus. The round voyage took fifty days.

John Jones sailed as a steward aboard that company's combination passenger-cargo ships, the *Hildebrand* and *Hubert*:

These voyages along the Amazon were hot, steamy, thickly humid. The crew would often sleep on deck. Below, if you opened a porthole, insects of all sizes and types would come flooding in! The ships' navigating officers had to be very careful because of submerged rocks and floating logs in the river. Once, we bent the ship's only screw and then limped to Manaus. There was no shipyard in such a remote place and so two Brazilian divers were hired to make repairs. They carved away some of the twisted steel but which actually made the ship faster than before. The chief engineer was more than surprised – and pleased! We carried businessmen, traders and sometimes even a few tourists in first class and missionaries, medical people and teachers in tourist class. The crew often bought parrots and birds in Manaus and then brought them home to Liverpool. Myself, I bought a little Cayman, kept it in my cabin, but then discovered it didn't like colder climates. Soon after landing in Liverpool, I gave it to the Chester Zoo. Liverpool customs were easy in those days. Give them a few pounds and almost anything could be brought in!

The 7,700grt *Hildebrand* was commissioned in 1951 and the slightly larger 8,000grt *Hubert* in 1955. Both ships were rather unusual for their time in having their superstructures placed farther aft than usual. They were both two-class ships, with the *Hubert*'s quarters divided between seventy-four first class and ninety-six tourist class. Unfortunately, the *Hildebrand* was wrecked off the Portuguese coast in September 1957. The aged *Hilary*, dating from 1931, assisted until 1961 when she was replaced at Booth by the Belgian *Thysville*, which sailed for three years on the Amazon run as the *Anselm*. The 439ft-long *Hubert* soldiered on until October 1964 when she was transferred with Booth's parent, the Blue Star group, to the Singapore-based Austasia Line, becoming the *Malaysia* for passenger-cargo service between western Australia and Singapore. In 1976, she was rebuilt as the livestock carrier *Khaleej Express*, flying Saudi Arabian colours on the Australia–Middle East trade. She went to Pakistani ship breakers in 1984.

CHARGEURS RÉUNIS

CLAUDE BERNARD AND *LAVOISIER*

The passenger-cargo liners of France's Chargeurs Réunis were, in the 1950s, largely overshadowed by the big liners of the French Line, the Compagnie Générale Transatlantique, such as the famed *Transat*, as well as, but to a lesser extent, by the passenger-carrying ships of Messageries Maritimes. I myself knew of the Chargeurs Réunis through the glossy pages of the late Laurence Dunn's encyclopaedic *Passenger Liners*, produced in 1961 and then updated in 1965. I do recall, however, the maiden arrival at New York in April 1965 of a flag-bedecked cruise ship – the *Viking Princess*. Owned by Norway's Viking Cruise Lines, the 600-berth ship was coming to New York to run cruises of between one and seven nights. Although a completely rebuilt ship, she was notable to me as she had been the *Lavoisier* of Chargeurs Réunis in her previous life.

Royal occasion: The smart-looking *Hildebrand* is dressed in flags as she represents the Booth Line at Queen Elizabeth II's Coronation Fleet Review in June 1953. (Booth Line)

Paris-based Chargeurs Réunis ran passenger services to three continents: the east coast of South America, French colonial Africa and French Indo-China. After the Second World War, the company opted to concentrate on combination liners rather than full passenger ships. Designed and ordered in 1945–46, the first pair – named after French scientists – was built at St Nazaire, 11,900 tons in size and fitted to carry ninety-four passengers in first class and 230 in third class (later revised to 147 in first class and 296 in third class). The *Lavoisier* was launched on 30 October 1948 and delivered in September 1950; the *Claude Bernard* was launched a day later, on 31 October 1948, but completed six months earlier than her sister, in March 1950. Two sisters followed, the *Laënnec* and *Charles Tellier*, but they were not delivered until 1952 and were assigned to the Compagnie de Navigation Sud-Atlantique (see pp.27–9).

The *Lavoisier* and *Claude Bernard* had rather fine French post-war quarters, with modern public rooms, partial air conditioning, a sun deck with pool, full private bathrooms in all-first-class cabins and private toilets in all third-class rooms. Along with the aforementioned *Laënnec* and *Charles Tellier*, and joined in 1952 by the slightly improved *Louis Lumière*, these five ships sailed in regular service. There was a sailing every two weeks from Hamburg, Antwerp and Le Havre, then stops in Vigo, Leixões (Portugal) and Madeira, then across to Rio de Janeiro, Santos, Montevideo and Buenos Aires. It took more than a decade, however, for the passenger trade to South America to decline. The *Lavoisier* and *Claude Bernard*, being the oldest, were the first to go.

The 537ft-long *Lavoisier* was withdrawn first, in 1961, and sold to otherwise unknown Italian buyers – Palermo-based Commerciale Maritima Petroli S.p.A. At a Genoa shipyard, they had the ship rebuilt thoroughly for 600 all-first-class cruise passengers. Renamed *Riviera Prima*, she became a virtually new ship with modern, Italian-styled public rooms, all cabins with facilities and a large lido with pool fitted in the stern. She was chartered mostly to American interests: to Caribbean Cruise Lines, based in New York, for three-night weekend cruises 'to nowhere', week-long voyages to Bermuda and Nassau, or longer journeys to Caribbean ports. Unfortunately, Caribbean Cruise Lines' operations were soon clouded with financial problems and by the autumn of 1964 the *Riviera Prima* was for sale.

Quickly purchased by Norwegian buyers Berge Sigval Bergesen of Oslo, she was improved further, modernised and renamed *Viking Princess* for a new affiliate company, Viking Cruise Lines. She was reintroduced to cruising in April 1965. Once again she was used in US cruising, but this time from a

The *Lavoisier* seen at Le Havre. (Alex Duncan)

wide variety of ports, including New York, Boston, Baltimore, Philadelphia, Norfolk and Port Everglades. Unfortunately, she was soon finished off by a problem faced by many French-built ships – fire.

On 8 April 1966, in subsequently headline-making news, the cruise ship *Viking Princess* caught fire and burned out off Cuba. The 12,000-ton ship was on a Caribbean cruise at the time. Captain Klaus Brecht was then serving aboard the freighter *Cap Norte*, a West German vessel, and raced to the rescue, recalling how, 'We rescued passengers and crew, but some of the crew were quite notorious. They seemed more interested with the monies and other valuables in the ship's safe.'

The fire started in the ship's engine room and spread quickly. An order to abandon ship was given quickly, and along with the *Cap Norte*, two other freighters – the *Chungking Victory* and *Navigator* – rushed to the rescue. The *Navigator* performed an added duty by towing the blistered, wrecked *Viking Princess* to Port Royal in Jamaica. Sadly, she had to be written off as a complete loss and was later towed to Bilbao in Spain for scrapping.

The *Claude Bernard* was sold off a year after her sister, in 1962, and passed to communist East German owners, Deutsche Seereederei. Renamed *J.G. Fichte*, she sailed on for another seventeen years before being sold, in 1979, to a Panama-flag holding company and renamed *Sunrise IV* and then *Pegancia*. Laid up in her final months, she was towed to Karachi in April 1981 and demolished.

COMPAGNIE

DES

MESSAGERIES MARITIMES

12, Boulevard de la Madeleine — PARIS (9ᵉ)

Tél   OPÉra 07-60 et RIChelieu 88-40

■

PAQUEBOT A MOTEURS

" LOUIS LUMIÈRE "

■

PLAN

EMMÉNAGEMENTS POUR PASSAGERS	PASSENGER ACCOMMODATION
PREMIÈRE CLASSE	FIRST CLASS
TROISIÈME CLASSE	THIRD CLASS

■

CARACTÉRISTIQUES

LONGUEUR (LENGTH)	163. m. 600 (537 ft)
LARGEUR (BREADTH)	20 M. 670 (68 ft)
DÉPLACEMENT (DISPLACEMENT)	17.630 T
VITESSE (SPEED)	17 nds (knots)
PUISSANCE (HORSE POWER)	12.000 CV. (HP)

A deck plan for the *Louis Lumière*, built in 1952. (Andrew Kilk Collection)

LOUIS LUMIÈRE

As the last ship of a series sometimes known as the 'French savant class', the *Louis Lumière* differed mostly in having a more modern, domed funnel. Delivered in October 1952, she too served on the North Europe–South America run. Accommodations on the 12,300-tonner were arranged for 109 in first class and 302 in third. She sailed for fifteen years until replaced, in 1967, by the brand-new *Pasteur* (qv). By then, South American had become part of another French shipowner, Marseilles-based Messageries Maritimes.

The 537ft-long *Louis Lumière* was sold, like several of her French fleet mates, to Compañia de Navegación Abeto, a Panama-flag holding company, which in turn chartered the ship to Indonesia's Arafat Lines, who purchased her specifically to carry Mulsim pilgrims to Jeddah. Renamed *Mei Abeto*, she was refitted with much enlarged passenger quarters – 415 cabin passengers and 622 pilgrims in deck class. Her movements were varied over the next decade or so and included bouts of mechanical trouble. She was finally laid up at Djakarta in July 1977 and then sold seven years later to Bangladesh ship breakers. The long-neglected and much rusted ship was delivered at Chittagong in May 1984.

CHINA NAVIGATION CO. LTD

ANKING AND ANSHUN

Even writing a letter to far-off Hong Kong seemed like an adventure for a 14-year-old schoolboy like me. It was 1962, and I mailed off a request to the China Navigation Co. Ltd offices in Hong Kong. Weeks later, there was a reply – a large envelope containing deck plans, sailing schedules and rate sheets for the combo liners *Changsha* and *Taiyuan*. There was little for the smaller *Anking* and *Anshun*, however, since these ships were used in the charter trades, often carrying Muslim pilgrims to and from Jeddah.

When China Navigation began its post-Second World War rebuilding programme in 1945, eighteen vessels were ordered and ten of these were passenger-cargo ships. Two of these ships, the *Anking* and *Anshun*, were intended specifically for the China coast–Singapore service carrying large numbers of Chinese labourers. They were designed with quarters for fifty cabin passengers and 1,000 tween deck. The *Anking* was built at Greenock, in Scotland, in 1950 while the *Anshun* was constructed a world away, at the

Taikoo Dockyard in Hong Kong. Changes followed, with the ships being used in Hong Kong–Pacific islands service as well as carrying religious pilgrims to and from Jeddah. They endured for some twenty years, with the *Anking* being sold in 1970 to the Singapore-based Straits Steamship Company, renamed as the *Klias*. Used in service to Borneo, she operated for another six years before being damaged while docking at Singapore in 1976 and soon after being sold for scrap. The *Anshun* lasted far longer. Sold in 1971 to Pakistan's Pan-Islamic Steamship Company and being renamed *Safina-E-Abid*, she sailed mostly in pilgrim service until broken up at Gadani Beach in 1991.

CHANGSHA AND TAIYUAN

The 7,412grt *Changsha* was China Navigation's largest ship and pride when she was delivered by Greenock shipbuilders in 1949. An identical sister, the 440ft-long *Taiyuan*, followed shortly thereafter. These ships were used on the long-haul run from Sydney, Melbourne to other Australian ports and to Okinawa and Hong Kong. Exceptionally spacious ships, they had berthing for forty first- and forty-two tourist-class passengers (later amended to eighty-two first-class and seventy third-class passengers). A prized amenity on board was the first-class dining room's air conditioning, a feature later extended to several first-class cabins as well.

Victim to airline competition as well as the rise of container shipping, the *Changsha* was sold off in 1969 to the Pacific International Lines, becoming the *Kota Panjang*. Mostly she traded between Hong Kong, Canton, Penang and Singapore, but she also made voyages with Chinese workers to and from East Africa. She was scrapped in Pakistan in 1981. Also acquired by Pacific International in 1972, the *Taiyuan* became the *Kota Sahabat*, for mostly tourist service between Australia and Fiji. That service failed, however, and the ship was refitted to carry Australian sheep to Middle East ports. The ex-*Taiyuan* was scrapped at Kaohsiung on Taiwan in 1980.

THESE SCHEDULES ARE FOR GUIDANCE ONLY.

AUSTRALIA/PORT MORESBY/MANILA/KEELUNG/HONG KONG/AUSTRALIA

	Melbourne	Sydney	Brisbane	Pt. Moresby	Manila	Keelung	Hong Kong	Brisbane	Sydney	Melbourne
Changsha 73	Nov 11	Nov 13–15	Nov 17–18	Nov 22–23	Nov 30/Dec. 2	Dec. 4–6	Dec. 8–16	Dec. 28–29	Dec. 31/Jan. 3	Jan. 5
Taiyuan 74	Dec. 10	*Dec. 15–17	Dec. 19–20	Dec. 24–26	Jan 2–4	Jan 6–7	Jan. 9–16	Jan 28–30	Feb. 1–3	Feb. 5
Changsha 74	Jan 10	Jan. 12–14	Jan. 16–17	Jan. 21–22	Jan 29–30	Feb. 1–2	‡Feb. 4–16	Feb. 28/Mar 1	Mar 3–4	Mar 6
Taiyuan 75	Feb. 11	Feb. 13–16	Feb. 18–20	Feb. 24–25	Mar 4–5	Mar 7–8	Mar. 10–16	Mar 28–29	Mar 31/Apr 3	Apr 5
Changsha 75	Mar 11	†Mar 17–20	Mar 22–23	Mar 27–28	Apr 4–5	Apr 7–8	Apr. 10–16	Apr 28–29	May 1–3	May 5
Taiyuan 76	Apr 11	†Apr 17–19	Apr 21–22	Apr 26–27	May 4–5	May 7–8	May 10–16	May 28–29	May 31/June 2	June 4
Changsha 76	May 12	†May 18–20	May 22–23	May 27–28	June 4–5	June 7–8	June 10–16	June 28–29	July 1–4	July 6
◆**Taiyuan** 77	June 7	June 9–10	June 12–12	June 16–16	June 23–24	June 26–26	‡Jun. 28/Ju 16	July 28–29	July 31/Aug. 2	Aug. 4
Changsha 77	July 13	July 15–19	July 21–22	July 26–27	Aug. 3–5	Aug. 7–8	Aug. 10–16	Aug. 28–29	Aug. 31/Sept. 2	Sept. 4
Taiyuan 78	Aug. 12	Aug. 14–19	Aug. 21–22	Aug. 26–27	Sept. 3–5	Sept. 7–8	Sept. 10–16	Sept. 28–29	Oct. 1–4	Oct. 6
Changsha 78	Sept. 11	Sept. 13–18	Sept. 20–21	Sept. 25–26	Oct. 3–5	Oct. 7–8	Oct 10–16	Oct. 28–30	Nov. 1–3	Nov. 5
Taiyuan 79	Oct. 13	Oct. 15–18	Oct. 20–21	Oct. 25–26	Nov 2–4	Nov 6–7	Nov. 9–16	Nov 28–29	Dec. 1–4	Dec. 6
Changsha 79	Nov 11	Nov 13–18	Nov 20–21	Nov 25–26	Dec. 3–4	Dec. 6–7	Dec. 9–16	Dec. 28–29	Dec. 31/Jan 4	Jan 6

*Calls Hobart   †Calls Nth. Tasmania   ‡Docks in Hong Kong   ◆No round trip passengers on this voyage.

Changsha/Taiyuan (7,500 tons) each carry 80 First Class Passengers. All Single and Two-Berth Cabins are air conditioned—some with private facilities. Three and Four-Berth Cabins are not air conditioned

A 1955 sailing schedule for the sisters *Changsha* and *Taiyuan*. (Andrew Kilk Collection)

Chinese style: The *Changsha* departing from Sydney with the famed Harbour Bridge in the background. (China Navigation Company)

Changing hands: The *Changsha* at sea but in her later life as the *Kota Panjang*. (Richard Faber Collection)

COMPAGNIE MARITIME BELGE

ALBERTVILLE, LEOPOLDVILLE, ELISABETHVILLE, BAUDOUINVILLE/THYSVILLE AND *CHARLESVILLE*

The Belgians had a strong link to Africa – on the colonial run to and from Congo. The routing was quite basic, from Antwerp to Matadi and then Lobito. After the Second World War and considerable losses, the Compagnie Maritime Belge – also known as the Belgian Line – ordered no less than five 10,900-ton combo liners from a national shipbuilder, the Cockerill shipyard at Hoboken. They were completed between 1948 and 1951 as the *Albertville*,

Leopoldville, Elisabethville, Baudouinville (renamed *Thysville* in 1957) and *Charlesville*. Moderate ships with top speeds of only 15½ knots, the first carried up to 207 one-class passengers while the last two had up to 248 berths. Each ship was fitted with a set of pleasant public rooms, a dining room, children's nursery (with separate play deck), a hairdresser and barber's shop, gift ship, sun deck and outdoor pool. Some cabins had either a toilet and private shower or bath.

After the larger, faster *Jadotville* and *Baudouinville* were added in 1956–57, the five earlier ships were re-engined, increasing service speeds to 16½ knots. Operating together, these seven Belgian combo ships operated for less than four years. After the Congo was granted political independence in the summer of 1960, the CMB passenger trade suddenly fell away. The 3-year-old *Jadotville* and *Baudouinville* were sold off almost immediately, becoming P&O's *Chitral* and *Cathay* respectively, followed by the *Thysville*, which was sold to Britain's Blue Star Line, becoming the *Iberia Star* (qv).

The *Albertville, Leopoldville, Elisabethville* and *Charlesville* continued for some years thereafter, running a fortnightly service from Antwerp and from Lobito and Matadi. In 1967, the *Leopoldville* was transferred to a new sister company, the Compagnie Maritime Congolaise and hoisted the colours of Zaire. She was renamed *P.E. Lumumba*. Soon afterward, further decline and disintegration followed. The *Charlesville* was sold off to the East Germans, to Rostock-based Deutsche Seereederei. Renamed *Georg Buchner*, her passenger quarters were put to good use carrying cadets for the East German merchant navy. She was finally laid up in 1977, used as museum ship at Rostock. She finally sank in May 2014 while en route to scrappers in Lithuania. Disaster also struck these five original sisters of the Belgian Line. On 20 March 1968, the *Elisabethville* burned whilst at her Antwerp berth and was badly damaged. Beyond economic repair, she was sold to ship breakers and partially scrapped at Antwerp and then at Ghent.

The last two ships saw almost twenty-five years of service. The *Albertville* was sold to Taiwanese scrappers in the spring of 1973 and the *P.E. Lumumba* was retired as well in 1973, but had a rather extended demolition afterward – first at Tamise, then at Ghent and finally, with her remaining hull under tow, to Rio Grande in Brazil.

BAUDOUINVILLE AND *JADOTVILLE*

This strikingly handsome pair of combo liners – with a capacity of 300 one-class passengers each – had very short careers with the Belgians. The 13,900grt *Baudouinville* was built by the Belgians themselves in 1957, and

Off to the colonial Congo: The *Baudouinville* departs from Antwerp in this view dated 26 October 1955. The 10,900grt ship was the first to use the New Lock. King Baudouin was aboard during the opening ceremonies. (Cronican-Arroyo Collection)

the *Jadotville* came from the French, being built at St Nazaire in 1956. Used on the Antwerp–Matadi–Lobito run, they were made redundant by Congo independence in 1960 and quickly sold off. Promptly, they found buyers, the P&O-Orient Lines, becoming the *Cathay* and *Chitral* (qv) respectively for London–Far East sailings. Allocated to P&O's Eastern & Australian Line in 1969–70, they sailed the Australia–Far East run for a few years. The *Chitral* (ex-*Jadotville*) was finally sold to Taiwanese scrappers in 1976 and the *Cathay* (ex-*Baudouinville*) was sold to the Chinese, becoming the *Shanghai* for the Hong Kong–Shanghai service until scrapped in 1996.

FABIOLAVILLE AND *KANANGA*

Although I have experienced more than a normal share of sea voyages, I regretted not taking advantage of an offer to sail from Antwerp to Tenerife aboard the seventy-one-passenger combo liner *Fabiolaville*. I had written to the Compagnie Maritime Belge offices in Antwerp, requesting materials and photos, and the responding officer was a passenger ship enthusiast. He knew of my work, my many books about passenger ships. He invited me to join a five-night passage aboard the *Fabiolaville*. I was intrigued, of course, but the dates did not work. I also remember the Belgian Line, as the company was

The subsequent newer, larger and more luxurious *Baudouinville*, commissioned in 1957, was sold to P&O in 1961 and became its *Cathay*. (Richard Faber Collection)

The *Fabiolaville* and her sister represented a new, more contemporary design for combo ships built in the 1970s and afterward. (Compagnie Maritime Belge)

At 13,481grt and with space for only seventy-one first-class passengers, their accommodation was arranged on three decks. The salon, bar, verandah, outdoor pool, children's playroom and several larger staterooms were located on the uppermost A Deck. Further cabins, all of which had private bathrooms, were located on B and C Decks. The restaurant was on the lower deck, which also included a small gift shop and a beauty salon. The passenger scheme was actually divided between fifty-eight adults and thirteen small children, and each ship was looked after by a crew of sixty-three. In their five holds, which had space for as many as 200 containers, the ships tended to carry conventional manufactured goods on the southbound runs and then return with the likes of cocoa, rubber, coffee, copper and cobalt.

The *Fabiolaville* was sold to Chinese buyers in 1989 and sailed as the *Hai Hua* until scrapped in 1999. The *Kananga* was sold off for tramp service to Liberian-flag owners in 1993, becoming the *Anang*, then *Chryso* and finally *Norbel Oman*. She was broken up in 1997.

COMPAGNIE DE NAVIGATION SUD-ATLANTIQUE

LAËNNEC AND *CHARLES TELLIER*

These ships were operated by Compagnie de Navigation Sud-Atlantique, an affiliate of the aforementioned Chargeurs Réunis. *Laënnec* and *Charles Tellier* were delivered in January and July of 1952 and used on the north Europe–east coast of South America service. They were fitted with passenger quarters for 110 in first class and 326 in third class.

After nearly fifteen years' service in the South Atlantic, they were made redundant and sold off. The *Laënnec* was sold off in 1966, going to Compañía de Navegación Abeto, which was based in Panama, but placed under charter to Indonesia's Arafat Lines. Renamed *Belle Abeto*, she divided her operations between carrying Muslim pilgrims between Djakarta and Jeddah, and ferrying passengers between Singapore, Hong Kong, Kobe and Yokohama. She had been extensively refitted with an increased capacity from some 400 to almost 1,500. Her new accommodations were listed as 100 in cabins and 1,352 pilgrims in deck class.

The *Charles Tellier* followed her sister to eastern waters, becoming the *Le Havre Abeto*. She too sailed for the Arafat Lines, in both pilgrim as well as Far Eastern services.

also known, from their offices in Lower Manhattan, on the upper floor of a building at 26 Beaver Street. In the reception lobby, there was a model of the combo liner *Albertville*, wonderfully detailed, highly accurate and resting in a glass and mahogany case.

While almost all other combination passenger-cargo liners had disappeared by the mid 1980s, two of the remainders, the sisters *Fabiolaville* and *Kananga*, ironically dated from an old colonial run that continued to thrive: the route between Belgium and Zaire, the former Belgian Congo. These two ships made regular sailings every three weeks between Antwerp and Matadi, with calls en route at Tenerife, Dakar and Abidjan.

Built at the Cockerill-Ougrée Shipyard at Hoboken in Belgium, the two identical ships were in fact owned and operated by separate firms, flying different flags. The *Fabiolaville* was registered to Compagnie Maritime Belge, the Belgian Line, and registered at Antwerp, while the *Kananga*, as her African-sounding name suggests, was owned by Compagnie Maritime Zaïroise of Kinshasa and showed Matadi as her homeport. These ships were designed as engine-aft replacements for the earlier Leopoldville class, which dated from the late 1940s and early '50s. The new ships were delivered in June 1972 and January 1973 respectively.

The interconnecting sitting room and bedroom of a suite, one of two, aboard the 12,007grt *Laënnec*. Altogether, the ship had 110 berths in first class. (Andrew Kilk Collection)

The first-class dining room aboard the 16-knot *Charles Tellier*. (Andrew Kilk Collection)

The smart but unpretentious look of the *Charles Tellier*. (Steffen Weirauch)

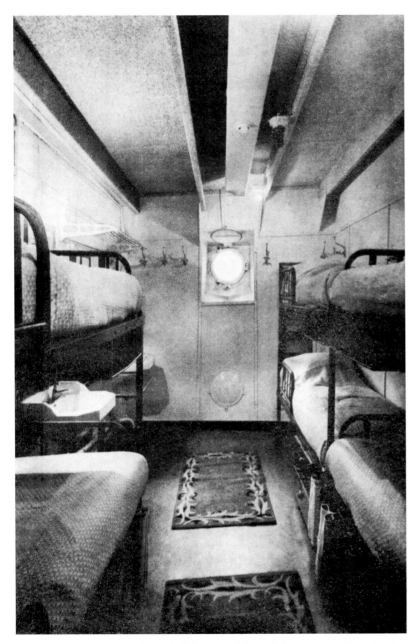

The simplicity of a six-berth cabin in third class aboard the 537ft-long *Laënnec*. Altogether, the ship carried up to 326 passengers in third class. (Andrew Kilk Collection)

The *Belle Abeto* (previously the *Laënnec*) was destroyed by fire, on 30 July 1976, while at Sasebo, Japan. She burned from end to end, became a total wreck and was later towed out to sea and sunk. The *Le Havre Abeto* (previously the *Charles Tellier*) was laid up soon afterward. Their trade had gone by then as the pilgrim business had switched to the airlines and there were new, strict regulations for Indonesian pilgrim ships. The *Le Havre Abeto* was laid up at Djakarta for several years, alongside the *Mei Abeto*, formerly her fleet mate *Louis Lumière*, but soon slipped into poor condition. They were later reported as being 'heavily rusted, windows smashed and with the general appearance of neglect'. The *Le Havre Abeto* was sold to Bangladesh breakers and was delivered at Chittagong on 20 May 1984.

COMPAÑÍA TRANSATLÁNTICA ESPAÑOLA

COVADONGA AND *GUADALUPE*

The Spanish never quite invested in big passenger ships for the otherwise obvious passenger link to North America, but instead relied on smaller, often older tonnage. At the end of the Second World War, the Compañía Transatlántica Española (the Spanish Line to English speakers) ran three pre-war-built passenger ships on the New York run: the *Habana*, *Magallanes* and *Marques de Comillas*.

In 1952, to bolster as well as improve its North Atlantic operations, the state-owned firm bought two cargo ships, the *Monasterio de la Rabida* and *Monasterio de Guadalupe*, then fitting out for another Spanish shipowner, the Empresa Nacional Elcano. Both ships were redesigned and converted to combination liners and became the *Covadonga* and *Guadalupe* respectively. The cargo areas were reduced and reworked, and passenger quarters with 349 berths were added (105 in first class and 244 in tourist class). These new sisters were commissioned in 1953, put on the New York run and rather abruptly replaced all of the earlier Spanish tonnage. They proved, in fact, to be the very last new passenger ships for their owners. In the late 1950s, twin 20,000-tonners, to be named *Samos* and *Silos*, were proposed. They would have offered far greater accommodations, aiming for a bigger share of the midatlantic tourist trade, with sixty in first class and 800 in tourist. However, the Spanish government refused to finance the project, particularly in view of intruding and increasing airline competition.

The 487ft-long *Covadonga* and *Guadalupe* worked a rather extensive service from Bilbao, Santander, Gijon, Vigo and Lisbon across to New York and then southward to Havana (or San Juan) and Vera Cruz. Julio Del Valle, who was traffic manager at Garcia & Diaz, the ships' New York agents, recalled these ships as being quite pleasant and profitable:

> They differed only in decor – the *Covadonga* being very Spanish in style, whereas the *Guadalupe* was more European modern. They served excellent continental cuisine in their first-class restaurants and ethnic menus in tourist class. In 1962–63, they carried the last groups of Catholic priests and nuns out of communist Cuba.

These two ships also provided a valuable cargo service. 'Each ship had space for 6,000 tons of freight,' added Del Valle. 'To America, they often carried mail, tinned fish, squid, octopus, wine, mercury, cork, lead, Spanish canned goods, olives and olive oil. Homeward, they carried coffee and tobacco from Mexico, sugar and more tobacco from Cuba and finally machinery, tin plate, steel and agricultural machinery from New York.'

By the early 1970s, after two decades of service, these Spanish sisters had become unprofitable. Their routing had been altered somewhat in later years to include calls at Norfolk and Miami, and occasionally US Gulf ports such as New Orleans. Their complements were sensibly reduced to seventy-five first-class passengers only. The passenger trade eventually vanished, however, and the cargo went instead aboard new, more efficient container ships.

The *Covadonga* was retired in December 1972 and was quickly sold off to breakers at Castellon, Spain. The *Guadalupe* – at first intended to be sold for conversion to an Indian Ocean pilgrim ship – followed three months later. She terminated completely the North Atlantic passenger services for the Spanish Line.

Happy occasion: The flag-bedecked *Covadonga* arrives on her maiden voyage, on 8 September 1953, in New York Harbor. She later berthed in Hoboken. (James McNamara Collection)

CUNARD LINE

MEDIA AND *PARTHIA*

Despite being sometimes overshadowed by the Cunard Line's larger, more famous liners (the *Queen Elizabeth*, *Queen Mary*, *Mauretania* and *Caronia*), the *Media* and *Parthia* were popular and important assets to the company during its busy post-war years. The 530ft-long *Media* and *Parthia* came to New York with almost year-round regularity, even in the depths of winter. Typically for ships carrying large amounts of freight, they had long stays in port – arriving on Saturdays and then departing six days later, mostly on Friday afternoons. They would depart precisely at 3.30 p.m. and, with school finished for the day, I would often be watching twenty or so minutes later as they passed the Hoboken waterfront. They always looked impeccable with their black hulls, white superstructures, brown masts and, most noticeable, the flat single funnels in Cunard black and distinctive orange-red.

Cunard's only combination passenger-cargo liners, the 13,345grt *Media* (delivered in August 1947) was the first brand-new passenger ship to be delivered after the war and the first to be fitted with stabilisers (1953), while the *Parthia* followed in April 1948. They maintained year-round Liverpool–New York crossings until 1961. After this, the *Media* was sold to the Italian Cogedar Line, and greatly rebuilt (for 1,200 passengers) on the Europe–Australia run as the *Flavia*. The *Parthia* switched to New Zealand Shipping Co., becoming their *Remuera* until 1965 and then joined Eastern & Australian Steamship Company as

After a late morning sailing from New York's Pier 92, the *Media* is seen outbound from a passing Staten Island ferry in the Lower Bay. (Richard Faber Collection)

The attractive lounge with stage and piano aboard the 250-berth *Parthia*. (Richard Faber Collection)

the *Aramac*. The *Flavia* (ex-*Media*), later used as a Costa Line cruise ship, was sold off in 1982 to Chinese buyers, becoming the *Flavian* and then *Lavia*, but then burnt out at Hong Kong in January 1989. After being salvaged, she was sold to Taiwanese scrappers in 1990. The *Aramac* (ex-*Parthia*) was demolished a numbers of years earlier on Taiwan, in 1970.

CURNOW SHIPPING CO.

ST HELENA (1963) AND *ST HELENA* (1990)

As something of a last vestige of long-distance British passenger ship service, the Curnow Shipping Co. began operating a passenger-cargo service between Avonmouth and Cape Town, and was used as a link to the island of St Helena beginning in 1978. Until 1990, the 3,100grt *St Helena*, a former Canadian coastal vessel refitted to carry eighty-eight passengers, was used, but she was then

Cosy quarters: The intimate cocktail bar aboard the *Parthia*. (Richard Faber Collection)

Tragic ending: The one-time cruise ship *Flavia*, the former *Media*, burned out at Hong Kong in January 1989 and was later scrapped. (South China Morning Post Ltd)

replaced by a brand-new ship of 6,700 tons. Built at Aberdeen in Scotland, this 128-bed ship continues in service but is limited to round trips from Cape Town.

DELTA LINE

DEL MAR, DEL NORTE AND DEL SUD

A very modern, advanced trio: built for the Delta Line, based in New Orleans, and carrying up to 120 passengers each in high-standard accommodations, they were completed in 1946–47 and used on the east coast of South America route until the early 1970s.

DODERO LINE

PRESIDENTE PERON/ARGENTINA, EVA PERON/URUGUAY AND 17 DE OCTUBRE/LIBERTAD

Argentina never quite entered the deep-sea passenger trades until after the Second World War. At the prompting of the Argentine government itself, one of the first steps was to order a trio of very fine combination passenger-cargo ships from the famed Vickers-Armstrong yard at Barrow-in-Furness. They emerged as three particularly handsome vessels.

Their original owners were the Buenos Aires-based Dodero Line, which was state owned and controlled. The trio was therefore given political names. The first was launched on 3 November 1948 as the *Presidente Peron*. The *Eva Peron* followed in August 1949 and then, in April 1950, it was the *17 de Octubre*, the date of the Perons' rise to power in Argentina.

Each ship, capped by sizeable single funnels, was some 12,500grt and 530ft in length. With 18-knot service speeds, their operations were coordinated on sailing every three weeks, from Buenos Aires or from London. The passage time between those two ports was sixteen days. Intermediate ports of call included Le Havre, Lisbon, occasionally Madeira and then, in South America, Rio de Janeiro, Santos and Montevideo.

The passenger accommodation was all first class. The *Presidente Peron* differed in that she had a full capacity of seventy-four, whereas the other two ships could accommodate up to ninety-six. They were high-standard ships in all ways. C.M. Squarey wrote:

With her dummy funnel and twin uptakes, the *Del Norte* is seen berthed at New Orleans. (Gillespie-Faber Collection)

They are ships of quality and quantity ... quantity in the generous space per passenger. Everything [about these ships] is of a liberal scale. The public rooms are all air conditioned. The dining room is done in shades of green while the main lounge is in a delightful, essentially English style. Accommodations also included a music room (also used for dancing), gymnasium, outdoor pool and deck space that can be used as an outdoor cinema. Amongst the cabins, all doubles have a private shower and toilet; all singles have a full bathtub.

After the fall of the Peron regime in 1955, the ships changed names: *Presidente Peron* to *Argentina*, *Eva Peron* to *Uruguay* and *17 de Octubre* to *Libertad*. Their owners also changed, to the Ultramar Line, and their sailings extended to include Hamburg. In the following years, there were other changes. Ships were repainted in a variety of funnel colours and the hull colouring changed from grey to black and finally to white. In 1962 there was one further ownership change, this time to the ELMA Lines (Empresas Lineas Maritimas Argentinas). Also in 1962, the *Argentina* made several trips to New York as a replacement for the fire-damaged *Rio Jachal*.

Prompted by the invasion of jet aircraft, passenger trades and steamship-line economics were changing all too quickly by the mid 1960s. It was decided to convert the *Libertad* and *Uruguay* to all-tourist-class ships, carrying 400 passengers each. The *Libertad* was converted in 1964 at Buenos Aires, but the changes for the *Uruguay* were cancelled. She and the *Argentina*

The seventy-four-passenger *Argentina* in the colours of ELMA Lines. (Gillespie-Faber Collection)

Given a priority in otherwise crammed British shipyards because of exchange rates at the time, the launching of Argentina's 12,677grt *Eva Peron* was watched by crowds of officials as well as workmen in this 1949 view. (Cronican-Arroyo Collection)

remained in their original format. Later changes went ahead, however: in 1966, both the *Uruguay* and *Argentina* were downgraded to all-cargo status and later made government voyages south to the bottom of Argentina and even to Antarctica with supplies and, using the former passenger quarters, sometimes carrying research teams. Finally decommissioned, both were broken up in Argentina in 1973. Teamed with the rebuilt *Rio Tunuyan*, the *Libertad* had ceased carrying regular passengers by the early 1970s, and went on to make Antarctic sailings as well. She was laid up in 1974, and then scrapped a year later at the Argentine port of Campana.

DONALDSON LINE

LAURENTIA AND *LISMORIA*

In 1948–49, Glasgow-based Donaldson Line converted two American-built Victory ships, the *Taos Victory* and *Medina Victory*, and refitted them with fifty-five first-class berths as the *Laurentia* and *Lismoria*. They were used on the Glasgow–Montreal run (but in winter to St John, New Brunswick and

Halifax or to the North American west coast via Panama). They endured until late 1966, when they were both briefly used as freighters before being sold and Donaldson itself being disbanded. The 8,300grt *Laurentia* was scrapped at Kaohsiung in the summer of 1967 and the *Lismoria* met her end the winter before in Spain.

A classic wartime-built Victory ship, Donaldson's *Laurentia* and her sister *Lismoria* were refitted for passenger-cargo sailings on the North Atlantic with extended superstructures. (Richard Faber Collection)

EAST ASIATIC CO. LTD

JUTLANDIA, FALSTRIA, SEALANDIA, MEONIA AND *LALANDIA*

These Danish flagships were almost eccentric-looking with as many as four masts but no obvious funnels (the exhausts were worked through the third mast). The 1934-built *Jutlandia* (8,542grt) was the largest and finest, with berths for sixty-nine all-first-class passengers, while the *Falstria* (1945), *Selandia* (1938), *Meonia* (1927) and *Lalandia* (1927) were somewhat smaller. Continuing until the early 1960s, they ran a long, port-intensive service, stopping at Copenhagen, Aarhus, Gothenburg, Oslo, Middlesbrough, Antwerp, Bremen, Hamburg, Rotterdam, Dover, Marseilles and Genoa via Port Said to Aden, Penang, Port Swettenham, Singapore, Bangkok and Saigon. They were all retired in the early 1960s and later scrapped.

With her rounded Maierform bow and the exhausts worked through pipes attached to the third mast, the 460ft-long *Jutlandia* and her similar East Asiatic fleetmates created distinctive appearances. (Alex Duncan)

Very popular with wintertime passengers heading for the sunny Caribbean, the *Camito* is seen at Southampton. (Roger Sherlock)

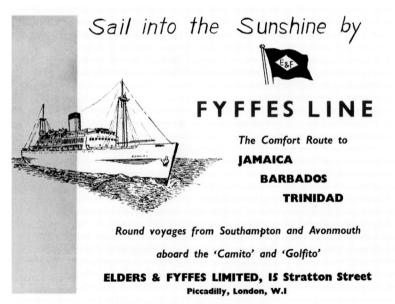

Winter voyages aboard the *Camito* and *Golfito* were often fully booked. (Fyffes Line)

ELDERS & FYFFES LINE

CAMITO AND *GOLFITO*

'Fifty years ago, back in the 1960s, it was a treat and rare privilege to be able to escape the cold, dreary, very dark English winter,' remembered Alice Carrender:

My grandmother invited me to join her on a four-week cruise of a kind – a trip on a 'banana boat'. It was not exactly a trip for a young girl in her twenties, but I really couldn't refuse. We sailed from Southampton on one of those cold, foggy, English winter days aboard the *Golfito*. She was a small ship, carrying only 100 or so passengers, but comfortable and inviting. We shared a cabin and had use of the lounge, library, ate three meals each day in the dining room and otherwise enjoyed the deck chairs surrounding the swimming pool. Most of the passengers were older, more my grandmother's age, and the crew were almost all British. I took the sun, read lots of books and felt the quiet excitement of this rather exotic journey for an otherwise English country girl.

We sailed to Trinidad, Barbados, Grenada, Kingston, Montego Bay and Bermuda. Cargo, mostly loading Fyffes bananas [the 8,000-ton *Golfito* was owned by the Fyffes Line], was the ship's main purpose, but there was always time in port for some sightseeing. We were the English ladies on tour – flowery dresses, sunhats and fringed parasols to shade from the hot sun. In the afternoons, my grandmother would nap in the stateroom and then rise in time for tea in the lounge. Dinner began late, at 8:30 p.m. as I recall, and was a rather long affair. We almost always dressed formally. It was all rather genteel, like staying in some old hotel. There were no cabaret shows or twelve-piece bands or even a cruise director. There was dancing, games like frog racing and film showings, which as I remember, were twice a week. It was a lovely opportunity for a young girl to sail the Caribbean in winter – but it was also like something from another age. Yes, genteel is the right word – that trip on the *Golfito* was genteel.

After the *Golfito* (1949) and *Camito* (1956) were retired in the early 1970s, Fyffes relied on freighters carrying six to twelve travellers for some years before abandoning passenger service altogether.

ELLERMAN & BUCKNALL LINE

CITY OF PORT ELIZABETH, CITY OF EXETER, CITY OF YORK AND *CITY OF DURBAN*

'To the well travelled, they ranked as the very best way to sail to South and East Africa from the UK,' recalled Peter Edwards, a frequent traveller on passenger ships to and from Africa. They were in fact the very last passenger ships in the once huge Ellerman fleet and were named *City of Port Elizabeth*, *City of Exeter*, *City of York* and *City of Durban*, and were built in 1952–54. Combination passenger-cargo ships at 13,300 tons and with 107 all-first-class berths, they were very popular ships, sailing regularly between London, Las Palmas, Cape Town, Port Elizabeth, East London, Durban, Lourenço Marques (now Maputo) and Beira. While on 'turnarounds' in the UK, these ships also called at Newcastle or Middlesbrough, Hamburg, Rotterdam and Antwerp to load additional cargo and also offer mini cruises.

After almost twenty years, the 541ft-long *City of York* made the last Ellerman Lines passenger sailing in June 1971. The quartet was sold to Greek owners, the Karageorgis Lines, all supposedly to be converted to high-standard Adriatic and Aegean ferries. With the sudden increase in fuel prices in 1973, however, plans soon changed, with the result that two of the ships were not converted. The *City of Durban*, which had become the *Mediterranean Dolphin*, was scrapped in 1974, while the *Mediterranean Island* (ex-*City of Port Elizabeth*) went to the breakers in 1980. The *City of Exeter* and *City of York* were lavishly converted as the high-standard ferries *Mediterranean Sea* and *Mediterranean Sky* respectively. The *Sea* sailed in her final days as the renamed *Alice* before being scrapped in 1999. The laid-up *Sky* sank at her moorings in Eleusis Bay, Greece, in November 2002.

FARRELL LINES

AFRICAN ENDEAVOUR AND *AFRICAN ENTERPRISE*

Beginning in the late 1940s, New York-based Farrell Lines not only had a large fleet of freighters, but two rather luxurious passenger-cargo liners, the 8,000grt *African Endeavour* and *African Enterprise*. They carried eighty-two passengers in superb quarters on fifty-six-day round-trip voyages between New York, Cape Town, Port Elizabeth, Durban, Lourenço Marques and Beira. The sixteen-night passage between New York and Cape Town was promoted to businessmen. Despite their fine service and clubby atmosphere, they were not very successful and were retired within ten years. After being laid up, both ships were sold to scrappers in 1969.

Among the finest combo liners of their day, the *City of Exeter* and her three sisters were hugely popular on the UK–South Africa run. They were often described as being like 'big yachts'. (Ellerman Lines)

SOUTH AFRICA
56-day Cruise

Regular sailings by the
distinguished sister ships

AFRICAN ENTERPRISE

AFRICAN ENDEAVOR

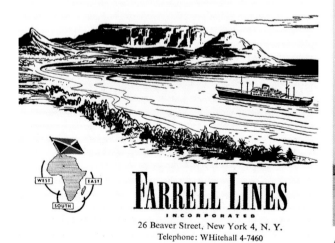

FARRELL LINES
INCORPORATED
26 Beaver Street, New York 4, N. Y.
Telephone: WHitehall 4-7460

Effective October 1, 1951 — Cancels all previous issues.

Above: American design: The *African Enterprise*, which had eighty-two passenger berths, is seen departing from Cape Town. (James McNamara Collection)

Left: Exotic routing: Voyages in the *African Endeavor* and *African Enterprise* were geared to one-way passenger traffic, but also complete fifty-six-day cruises. (Andrew Kilk Collection)

Above: Arriving at Boston, the *Nova Scotia* and her sister provided a rather unique North Atlantic passenger service. (Alex Duncan)

FURNESS WARREN LINE

NEWFOUNDLAND AND *NOVA SCOTIA*

These 7,400-ton sisters, built in the late 1940s, ran regular service for the Furness Warren Line between Liverpool, St John's (Newfoundland), Halifax and Boston. They carried sixty-two first- and ninety-two tourist-class passengers. Sold to become the *Francis Drake* and *George Anson* for Australia–Far East service of the Dominion Far East Line, they were both scrapped in 1971.

GLEN LINE

BRECONSHIRE, GLENARTNEY, GLENEARN, GLENGYLE, GLENORCHY, DENBIGHSHIRE, GLENGARRY AND *GLENROY*

Richard Remnant first went to sea in 1966. He was young and rather typically wanted to see the world. He signed aboard as an engineering officer with the Glen Line, then still a big British cargo ship operator. He had been told that the run out to the Far East was the most exciting and so Glen was ideal:

> I was assigned to the *Glenorchy*, then a big freighter, but an aged ship. She'd been built in the 1940s. She used to carry up to eighteen passengers, but this had been closed down and the officers were then using the passenger cabins. There were fourteen officers and seventy crew, and so a very large eighty-four crew altogether. In the officers' mess, there were two menus: European and Eastern. The food, as I remember, was very good.
>
> We had five days to load in London's King George V Dock before we set off on a ten-day swing around ports for loading – Hamburg, Rotterdam, Antwerp and, for the main cargo, at Birkenhead, just across from Liverpool. Then it was deep sea. We sailed direct, by way of the Suez Canal, to Penang in Malaysia. It took twenty-six days and that was our first port of call. Afterward, we called at Singapore and Manila, where we loaded eighty prime breeding pigs bound for China. There were kept on the fore deck and had to be kept fed. We delivered them to Shanghai, where the Red Guard official found a documentation error. As a result, one of our officers was interrogated for fourteen hours!
>
> On our return voyage, we stopped in tropical Borneo … There was no air conditioning and so the ship was sweltering, like an inferno. We were also invaded by flies, but a kind which were as big as a man's hand. They had to be scraped off the walls after they'd been sucked into the ship's fans and killed.

A powerful-looking ship: The UK-Far East routed *Denbighshire* and her sisters could carry up to eighteen passengers in comfortable quarters. (Alex Duncan)

> Like many other ships calling in Borneo, we loaded lots of palm oil. Loading the six holds was a work of art. It was all done very carefully and systematically. We also carried cargo in the tween decks. But on freighters, we actually carried every sort of cargo – from Austin taxis to toilet bowls, and once I even remember 10 tons of Indian hairnets.

These ships, eventually outmoded by the worldwide shift to containers, were retired and then broken up beginning in the late 1960s.

GRACE LINE

SANTA CLARA, SANTA MONICA, SANTA SOFIA, SANTA BARBARA, SANTA CECILIA, SANTA ISABEL, SANTA LUISA, SANTA MARIA AND *SANTA MARGARITA*

Based in New York, the Grace Line built nine combo liners just after the Second World War, in 1946. The first three of these fifty-two-passenger ships traded between New York and the Caribbean. The other six sisters were assigned to a longer service, from New York to ports along the west coast of South America. These ships endured until the late 1960s and subsequently finished up on tramping routes before going for scrap.

Friday morning sailing for South America: The *Santa Isabel* is outbound in the Hudson River with the similar *Santa Sofia* and the cruise ship *Nassau* in the background. (James McNamara Collection)

Morning operations: Inbound from the Caribbean, two Dalzell Towing Company tugs assist the 584ft-long *Santa Rosa* to her berth at Pier 57, West 15th Street, in Manhattan. (Richard Faber Collection)

SANTA ROSA AND *SANTA PAULA*

On Fridays in the 1950s and '60s, the proud passenger liners of the once very popular Grace Line departed. With steam whistles sounding, the sisters *Santa Rosa* and *Santa Paula* alternated their departures for the warm waters of the Caribbean. They ran thirteen-night itineraries, calling at Curaçao, La Guaira, Aruba, Kingston, Port-au-Prince and Port Everglades, Florida. Splendid ships that were yacht-like with intimate quarters with only a mere 300 passengers, they departed from Pier 57 in New York City. Located at the foot of West 15th Street in the city's now much gentrified Chelsea section; these days the pier has seen happier and certainly better days.

By 2010, the exterior of Pier 57 was scarred and rusting in places, 'graffiti artists' had done some work and numerous broken windows hinted at closure and abandonment. With its gleaming, stainless façade facing onto the mighty Hudson, the 900ft-long terminal might see better, renewed days in the future. There are plans to convert the city-owned property into a complex with a museum, shops, food markets, small theatres and other public spaces. Costs of a renewal of this type range from $200 to nearly $500 million.

In its day, the pier was an engineering marvel and a highlight to an otherwise ageing, worn city waterfront. The adjacent Chelsea piers dated from 1907–10. The earlier Pier 57, used until the 1930s by the French Line, burned down in 1947 and so had to be replaced. The steamship business was booming and Manhattan boasted of no fewer than 100 operative piers jutting out like fingers. The new Pier 57 was built on a trio of floating, concrete caissons that were actually constructed upriver, at Haverstraw, New York and then, in the care of a fleet of tugs, floated down the Hudson. The technology used in the pier had been inspired by the floating caissons used for beach landings in the Second World War.

The new Grace Line terminal formally opened in February 1954 and was highlighted not only by the most advanced cargo-handling methods (Grace Line had over two dozen ships, mostly freighters, in its US–Latin America services) as well as the novelty of rooftop parking for both passengers and staff. Grace occupied adjoining Pier 58 as well and, wishing to avoid dockers' overtime at weekends, no less than four Grace Line ships usually departed before 5 p.m. on Friday afternoons.

But business, as well as shipping, was changing by the 1960s, especially with the inception of speedy container operations. Grace moved south to Pier 40, at West Houston Street and shared with the likes of the Holland–America, Norwegian America and German Atlantic lines, in 1969. Pier 57 was transferred over, to a non-shipping role, to the City's Metropolitan Transportation Authority (MTA) for use as a bus garage and maintenance

facility. Finally moving out in 2004, the three-storey pier has been empty ever since. With renovation and restoration plans under further review, Pier 57 is due to reopen in 2015.

The *Santa Rosa* and *Santa Paula*, constructed in 1958, were the Grace Line flagships. Carrying 300 passengers in high-standard accommodations, they continued until the early 1970s. The 584ft-long *Santa Rosa*, after a long lay up at Baltimore, was sold to Greek buyers in 1989 and later rebuilt as the 960-berth cruise ship *Regent Rainbow*. She was sold again, in 1995, to Louis Cruise Lines, also Greek, and renamed the *Emerald*. She went to the breakers in 2012. The *Santa Paula* was sold in 1972 to the Sun Line, also Greek. The intention was to rebuild her as an Aegean cruise ship under the name *Stella Polaris*. These plans never materialised and instead she was later converted by Marriott Hotels for use as a moored hotel out in Kuwait. Renamed *Kuwait Mariott Hotel* and later *Ramada Al Salaam Hotel*, she was bombed and set afire in February 1991 during the Gulf War. Her remains were later demolished.

SANTA MAGDALENA, SANTA MARIA, SANTA MARIANA AND SANTA MERCEDES

To bolster its New York–west coast of South America service, Grace built four combo liners in 1963–64 with 125 passenger berths and self-handling containerised cargo space. Later operated by the Delta Line on the Around South America service but from North American west coast ports, they proved uneconomic and were retired in 1984. The *Magdalena*, *Maria* and *Mariana* were sold to Taiwanese breakers two years later. The *Mercedes* sailed on as the merchant marine training ship *State of Maine* until broken up in 2010.

Final fittings: The fifty-two-passenger *Santa Maria* poised in dry dock for final fitting out, at the Bethlehem Steel Shipyard on 56th Street in Brooklyn. The date is 12 September 1946. (James McNamara Collection)

Sleek in design and with just a pipe for smoke exhausts, the *Santa Mariana* and her sisters were designed for partial container cargo operations. (Grace Line)

Work under way: The 547ft-long *Santa Magdalena*, the first of four new sister ships for the Grace Line, is seen being completed at the Bethlehem Steel Shipyard at Sparrows Point, Maryland. This photo is dated 5 November 1962. (James McNamara Collection)

HAMBURG AMERICA LINE/ NORTH GERMAN LLOYD

FRANKFURT, HAMBURG, HANNOVER, BAYERNSTEIN, HESSENSTEIN AND SCHWABENSTEIN

At the end of the Second World War, the once mighty Hamburg America Line and North German Lloyd were all but totally depleted, being left with little more than very small coastal ships and harbour craft. Germany was in ruins and any form of rebuilding was under strict Allied control. Gradually, they did rebuild, but only small cargo ships at first. The first passenger ships were not constructed for almost ten years, until 1953–54, and surprisingly not for the prestigious North Atlantic trade to New York but for the far more extensive run to the Far East. Six passenger-cargo liners, three for each firm, were ordered from the Bremer Vulkan Shipyard at Bremen: the *Frankfurt, Hamburg* and *Hannover* for the Hamburg

American Line and the *Bayernstein, Hessenstein* and *Schwabenstein* for North German Lloyd.

At 9,000 tons each, they had high-standard passenger quarters arranged on four decks for a maximum of eighty-six passengers each. All staterooms had private bathroom facilities. The public rooms, done in contemporary and elegant styles, included a main lounge, reading-writing room, cocktail bar, glass-enclosed promenade, winter garden and dining room. There was also a pool on deck.

The six ships were routed on a ninety-five-day round-trip itinerary, sailing from Hamburg, Bremerhaven, Antwerp, Rotterdam and Southampton to Genoa, Port Said, Djibouti, Penang, Singapore, Hong Kong, Yokohama, Shimizu, Nagoya and Kobe before reversing course and repeating the same ports. Captain Heinz-Dieter Schmidt, whose father was master of the *Hessenstein*, stated:

Each of these ships had very deluxe accommodation. Fifty per cent of their passengers were Germans; the others were various Europeans and many British military and colonial civil servants. The ships worked on a three-and-a-half-month schedule, with one sailing each week from northern Europe, rotating between one passenger-cargo liner and one twelve-passenger freighter. Of course, cargo was very much a part of the livelihood of a ship such as the

The combination writing room-library aboard the *Bayernstein*. (Hapag-Lloyd)

One of West Germany's first passenger-cargo liners following the Second World War, the 8,974grt *Hannover* carried up to eighty-six passengers in luxuriously comfortable accommodation. (Alex Duncan)

Hessenstein. Altogether, there were six holds for 10,000 tons of freight: general cargo outwards and items such as rubber, coconut oil (there was a special tank onboard for up to 1,500 tons), latex, textiles and the beginnings of the mass-produced goods from Japan and Hong Kong on the homeward voyages.

Ships like the *Hessenstein* were outmoded by the mid '60s ... They were retired and sold off, to the giant C.Y. Tung group. A new, faster 22-knot Westphalia class of freighters took over the Far Eastern service. My father, who had commanded the *Hessenstein*, was then at the helm of the new *Hessenstein* in 1967.

Placed under the Liberian flag, for Tung's Orient Overseas Line, the ships were renamed respectively *Oriental Hero*, *Oriental Inventor*, *Oriental Warrior*, *Oriental Lady*, *Oriental Musician* and *Oriental Ruler* (qv).

HAMBURG–SOUTH AMERICA LINE

SANTA INES, SANTA TERESA, CAP SALINAS, SANTA ELENA, SANTA ISABEL & SANTA URSULA

After the Second World War, the once mighty German passenger liner fleet was in ruins. There were few survivors, in fact, with some ships going as reparations to the British, others to the Soviets and, largest of all, the 50,000-ton *Europa* to the Americans (but then soon allocated as reparations to the French, to later become the celebrated *Liberté*). There were two distinct transatlantic liner runs: the Hamburg America Line and the North German Lloyd, combined in the early 1930s as Hapag-Lloyd, looked after the northern run to New York; the Hamburg–South America Line covered the southern waters, to the east coast of South America.

Amidst very strict Allied limitations, the German fleet was allowed to be very slowly rebuilt in the early 1950s. Compared with the fine liners they had before the war, such as the superb, three-funnel *Cap Arcona*, the new ships they were permitted to build were modest. They built six combination passenger-cargo ships, each carrying up to twenty-eight all-first-class

The 6,982grt *Santa Isabel*, built in 1951 for the Hamburg–South America Line, could carry up to twenty-eight passengers in high-standard quarters. (Hamburg–South America Line)

passengers, for the long-haul run from Hamburg to Rio, Montevideo and Buenos Aires, with stops en route at Bremen, Rotterdam, Antwerp and then Las Palmas in the Canaries. Handsome-looking ships capped by red and white funnels, they had splendid passenger quarters decorated in rather opulent Edwardian styles. There was a fine-dining room, smoking room, bar and a small swimming pool on the otherwise small sun deck. Rather uniquely for the time, all of the staterooms had a private bathroom. The *Santa Ines* and *Santa Teresa* were slightly larger at 9,000 tons and 479ft in length. The *Cap Salinas*, *Santa Elena*, *Santa Isabel* and *Santa Ursula* were smaller at 7,200 tons. Diesel-driven with single screws, they were quite slow, managing a mere 13 knots at top speed.

Captain Klaus Schacht was then employed aboard the ships of Hamburg-Sud, as it was dubbed:

The *Santa Ursula* and her sisters were marvellous vessels. They had great interiors. They were always full with passengers. Germany had a huge link with

Changing hands: In later years, beginning in 1961, the 1953-built *Santa Teresa* sailed as the Pakistani-owned *Rustom*. In her original German configuration, she carried up to twenty-eight all-first-class passengers as well as a crew of fifty-four. (Steffen Weirauch)

Argentina in particular and trade was always very, very strong. For cargo, there was German and other European industrial goods going to South America and then returning with skins, meats, coffee, fertilisers and lots of special oils made from South American beans. We also carried vegetable oils in tanks. Hamburg–South America Line was one of the great merchants of Hamburg.

'These ships were exceptional for their time and were designed by Professor Pinnau, a noted interior architect who had worked for the Nazis in the 1930s. He had designed many buildings in the post-war port of Hamburg,' Captain Schacht remembered:

One passenger cabin on board the *Santa Catarina* was equal to the captain's cabin, but was especially for use by the German ambassador. These ships had Chippendale interiors and great libraries. There was a doctor on board and two ladies ran the laundry. There were five cooks and as many stewards to look after the passengers. The walls were adorned with old maps. The ships were slow by today's standards, making only 14 knots at top speed, but could reach Rio from Hamburg in three weeks. They called at Antwerp and then the Canary Islands and at Bahia on their way to Rio, Santos, Montevideo and finally Buenos Aires. I do remember that most of the stewards and cooks were also great smugglers of goods to and from South America. All of them made small fortunes back in the 1950s.

Outmoded by the 1960s, the Hamburg-built ships were sold off, mostly to become pure cargo ships. These days, Hamburg-Sud is a hugely successful container cargo ship operator, still sailing to South America, but without passengers.

HENDERSON LINE

PROME AND *SALWEEN*

These 7,000grt sisters carried seventy-six passengers each on the colonial run to and from Burma (Liverpool via Port Said, Port Sudan, Aden and Colombo to Rangoon). Both endured until 1962 when they were sold for scrapping.

HOLLAND–AFRICA LINE

JAGERSFONTEIN AND *ORANJEFONTEIN*

The Holland–Africa Line, once a mighty shipping company with numerous ships whose names ended in 'fontein' and 'kerk', was part of the United Netherlands Steamship Company, which by the 1980s was absorbed into the big Nedlloyd Group and was later swallowed up by the giant Maersk Line, the world's biggest container cargo ship operator by 2014. In its original form, Holland–Africa operated passenger-cargo liners on the North Europe–South and East Africa run. Their passenger operation had a very good reputation.

Two passenger-cargo liners were ordered in 1939, just before the Second World War erupted. The first of these, the *Rietfontein*, was laid down at the Schichau Shipyards, but just before launching, on 30 March 1940, the 528ft-long vessel was renamed *Elandsfontein*. The incomplete ship was soon seized by the Nazi forces that now occupied Poland. She was to have been completed for Hitler's navy, but then, rather strangely, was not finished and sat out the war in an incomplete state. On 14 March 1945, having been moved to Gdynia, she was damaged in an air attack and left to sink in the mouth of the Vistula. The battered Dutch were desperate for tonnage after the war in Europe ended, in May 1945, and sent a team from Amsterdam to Gdynia to inspect the badly damaged hull. It was two years before, on 30 March 1947, the hull was raised and taken to a Gdynia shipyard for patching and temporary repairs. She left Gdynia five months later, on 9 August, in the care of a seagoing tug, for the slow, very cautious tow to the De Schelde Shipyard at Vlissingen in Holland. To discard memories of the war, she was renamed, receiving her third name before even being completed, as the

An aerial view of the *Jagersfontein*. (Holland–Africa Line)

Jagersfontein. There was a shortage of shipyard crews as well as materials and it took another two years before the 10,500grt ship was ready, in March 1950, to enter commercial service to Africa. Her service ran from Hamburg to Mozambique via Amsterdam, Antwerp and Southampton to Cape Town, Port Elizabeth, East London, Durban and Lourenço Marques.

Sister ship to the 17-knot, twin-screw *Jagersfontein*, the *Oranjefontein* was ordered in 1939 as well, but from a Dutch shipbuilder, P. Smit, jun. at Rotterdam. She was launched in the spring of 1940 and completed that December, only to be transferred to the German navy. She was damaged in the Allied air attacks on Rotterdam on 28 April 1941. Later repaired, she was to have been managed by the German–Africa Line, but seems to have done very little actual sailing and instead was used in target practice by the German navy and air force. Later, in the winter of 1945, as the war was drawing to a close, she was to be renamed *Pioneer* and used in the Baltic for the evacuation of the Eastern Territories. This never happened, and instead she survived the war and was returned to the Dutch and then to the Holland–Africa Line. By September 1945, she was repaired and sailing – carrying Dutch nationals home from the colonial Caribbean outposts and making at least one sailing to the North American west coast via the Panama Canal. In 1946, having been fully restored, she entered African passenger service, carrying 160 passengers (100 in first class and 60 in tourist class).

They were quite delightful ships. C.M. Squarey wrote of them, 'I liked particularly the panelled ceiling, the parchment walls and the distinctive high-backed chairs in the Smoking Room; the Cocktail Lounge is certainly a room with "barsonality"; while the Main Lounge has a gentle, captivating charm of its own.' Almost all of the first-class staterooms had private facilities. There was a partially enclosed promenade deck and the sun deck included a swimming pool. Squarey added, 'Holland Africa has long enjoyed an enviable reputation and these ships [*Jagersfontein* and *Oranjefontein*] will not merely uphold it, but enhance it.'

The two ships lasted until 1967, when the passenger trade to Africa was already in slow but steady decline. The *Jagersfontein* was sold to Greek buyers and renamed *Devon*, but was then quickly resold to Taiwanese ship breakers. The *Oranjefontein* was sold directly to Spanish scrappers, who sailed her out to Bilbao as the *Fontein*.

RANDFONTEIN

A smart-looking ship, Holland–Africa's biggest and finest passenger-cargo liner was the 13,700-ton *Randfontein*, added in January 1959. Built by Wilton–

Evolution: The larger, better-appointed *Randfontein* of 1958 is seen at Cape Town. (Holland–Africa Line)

Fijenoord at Schiedam in Holland, she had a sizeable cargo capacity including special tanks for vegetable oils and refrigerated spaces for northbound South African fruits. Passenger quarters aboard the 584ft-long ship were divided between 123 in first class and 166 in tourist class. Each class had its own public areas as well as outdoor pool. All first-class cabins had private facilities and air conditioning extended to dining rooms and staterooms in both classes.

The *Randfontein* worked a sixty-five-day round-trip schedule: Hamburg, Amsterdam, Antwerp and Southampton via Tenerife to Cape Town, Port Elizabeth, East London, Durban and Lourenço Marques. In 1966, a round-trip fare started at £408 in first class and £252 in tourist class.

After the *Jagersfontein* and *Oranjefontein* were retired in 1967, the *Randfontein* was the sole passenger-cargo liner for Holland–Africa and was partnered with ten twelve-passenger freighters. The passenger trade dried up all but completely, however, and so the *Randfontein* was withdrawn in April 1971. That summer, she found further employment with another Dutch shipowner, the Royal Interocean Lines, and was renamed *Nieuw Holland*. Her new assignment: a triangular Pacific Ocean service (with passengers) from Sydney and Melbourne to Yokkaichi, Kobe and Yokohama, and then homeward via the Pacific islands. This was a rather short-lived phase in the ship's career – within three years, by 1974, she was sold and raised the flag of the People's Republic of China, becoming the *Yu Hua* and now home-ported at Canton. Her first assignment was carrying Chinese engineers, technicians and workers as well as supplies to East Africa, for a large railway project in Tanzania. Once that project was completed, she returned to regular passenger service, but on a far shorter route – crossing between Shanghai and Hong Kong. In 1981, she was renamed *Hai Xing*. She sailed for another fifteen years before going to Indian ship breakers in 1996.

HOLLAND–AMERICA LINE

NOORDAM AND *WESTERDAM*

Noted for their splendid and immaculate quarters, Holland–America Line had a great interest in passenger-cargo ships. They used the 148-passenger *Noordam* (1938) and 134-berth *Westerdam* (1946) on the Rotterdam–New York run.

DALERDYK AND *DONGEDYK*

Holland–America ran an alternate transatlantic service to the North American west coast, from north European ports via the Caribbean and Panama Canal to Los Angeles, San Francisco, Oakland, Portland, Seattle, Victoria and Vancouver. Two ships built before the war, the 10,900-ton sisters *Dalerdyk* and *Dongedyk*, carrying approximately fifty passengers each, assisted.

One of the earlier transatlantic combo liners, Holland–America's 10,700grt *Noordam*, commissioned in 1938, carried up to 150 one-class passengers on nine-day passages between New York and Rotterdam. (Holland–America Line)

DIEMERDYK AND *DINTELDYK*

The larger vessels on Holland–America's west coast service were the near sisters *Diemerdyk* (1950) and *Dinteldyk* (1957), which carried sixty passengers in superb accommodations. The *Diemerdyk* had the distinction of being the very first Holland–America Line ship to be built in Holland after the war.

Outbound for Europe: The 1950-built *Diemerdyk* passes under the Lions Gate Bridge at Vancouver. (Alex Duncan)

Banner day: The similar *Westerdam* is berthed along the outer end of brand-new Pier 40, in New York. The larger *Nieuw Amsterdam* is on the left with the *Oranje* to the right. (Port Authority of New York & New Jersey)

Different from her Holland–America fleet mates in North American west coast service, the 504ft-long *Dinteldyk* was painted with a dove-grey hull colouring. She carried up to sixty passengers, all in outside cabins and all with private bathroom facilities. (G. Monteny)

Brand new: Minus containers stowed on her fore decks, the *Americana* arrives in New York Harbor on her maiden call. (Ivaran Lines)

INDO-CHINA STEAM NAVIGATION CO. LTD

EASTERN QUEEN

Operated by the Hong Kong-based Indo-China Steam Navigation Co. Limited, the 8,644grt *Eastern Queen*, built in 1950, carried up to twenty-six first-class passengers (as well as deck-class passengers) on the Japan–Hong Kong–Australia run.

IVARAN LINES

AMERICANA

Built by Hyundai in South Korea in 1988, this 19,203grt vessel was initially intended as the first of three passenger-container cargo ships (the others were to be the *Brasilia* and *Argentina*). Carrying up to 110 travellers in luxurious quarters (and 1,200 containers), she was used by Norwegian-flag *Ivaran* on the US east coast–east coast of South America run. It was all rather short-lived. Finishing in combo service in 1999, she then went in the tramp trades as the much diminished *Golden Trade*. This once luxurious combo ship finished her days, at the age of 22, in a Chinese scrapyard in the winter of 2010.

ALCOA
to the Caribbean
FROM NEW ORLEANS

JAMAICA
DOMINICAN REPUBLIC
CURACAO
LA GUAIRA-FOR CARACAS
PUERTO CABELLO
GUANTA
TRINIDAD

ss EXETER
ss EXCALIBUR

AMERICAN EXPORT LINES

Above: Post-war style: American Export Lines' 'Four Aces' were the very first fully air-conditioned passenger ships. They were commissioned in 1948. (Author's Collection)

Left: Tropic destinations: *Alcoa* cruises to the Caribbean. (Andrew Kilk Collection)

Right: The 595ft-long *Savannah* was intended to show the use of nuclear-powered propulsion for merchant ships under the US flag. (Author's Collection)

Comfort at sea: The dining room aboard the sixty-passenger *Savannah*. (Author's Collection)

The luxurious Lounge can double as a movie theater

The Main Lobby looking toward the Purser's Square.

The spacious Veran opens onto the Swimming Pool

1960s modern: Passenger spaces aboard the $60 million *Savannah*. (Author's Collection)

Circumnavigation: Around the world aboard the ninety-five-passenger *President Monroe* and *President Polk*. (Andrew Kilk Collection)

AMERICAN PRESIDENT LINES

ROUND
THE
WORLD

S S PRESIDENT POLK · S S PRESIDENT MONROE

Sailings at 5 p.m. on Fridays: The three Rio liners of the Argentine State Line. (Author's Collection)

Especially popular with Australians, the *Centaur* offered a unique passenger-cargo service to and from Singapore. (Andrew Kilk Collection)

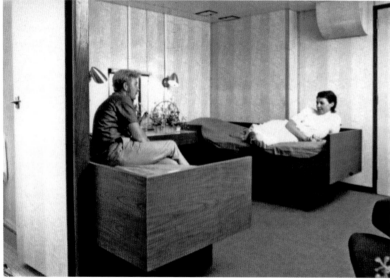

Pleasant quarters aboard the 190-bed *Centaur*. (Andrew Kilk Collection)

Spanish style: Transatlantic crossings on the two-class *Covadonga* and *Guadalupe*. (Andrew Kilk Collection)

WELCOME ABOARD! Your trip to Spain begins the moment you board the MS Guadalupe or MS Covadonga, two of the most comfortable and modern liners in service today.

From the captain to your personal steward, the entire crew is dedicated to making your voyage a most memorable and pleasurable experience— just like your visit to Spain itself For indeed, these deluxe liners are Spain afloat The decor, the cuisine the gracious service and warm smiles are all typical of Spanish hospitality.

You feel it the first time you step on deck. and you know right then that the sun and fun and easy living of the next few days represent the best travel investment you've ever made. And you're right, because knowledgeable travellers call the Guadalupe and Covandonga two of the best travel bargains on the seven seas.

NUEVA YORK   LA CORUÑA   GIJON   SANTANDER BILBAO

Good care under the watchful eye of Spanish officers and crew aboard the Spanish Line. (Andrew Kilk Collection)

Glasgow-based Donaldson Line ran the fifty-five-passenger *Laurentia* and *Lismoria* in seasonal service between Glasgow and Montreal. (Author's Collection)

CANADA SCOTLAND
DIRECT
Donaldson Line

The eighty-eight-berth *St Helena*, the former *Northland Prince*, offered service to the South Atlantic. She is seen in service during the Falklands War in 1982. (St Helena Shipping Co.)

The main lounge aboard the *Laurentia*. (Author's Collection)

A new *St Helena* was added in 1988. (Author's Collection)

Cosy quarters: A double-bedded room with private facilities aboard the one-class *Laurentia*. (Author's Collection)

RMS ST. HELENA

Plan of Passenger Accommodation

U.K. St. Helena R.S.A. St. Helena Shipping Co. Ltd.

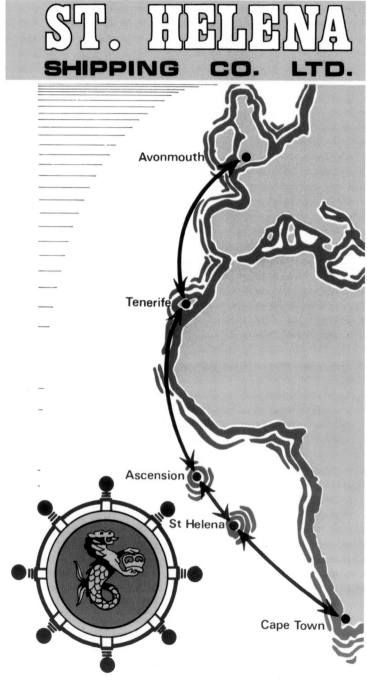

Far left: The *St Helena* offered unique voyages. (St Helena Shipping Co.)

Left: The southern route. (Author's Collection)

Loading cargo: Ellerman combo ships called at north European ports including Rotterdam. (Ellerman Lines)

The *Alice* being scrapped at Aliaga in Turkey in 1999. She had been the *City of Exeter* and later the rebuilt *Mediterranean Sea*. (Selim San)

Popular with business travellers, the Farrell Lines' passenger service to south and east Africa included seventeen-day voyages between New York and Cape Town. (Author's Collection)

CAMITO
GOLFITO

FYFFES LINE
TRINIDAD
JAMAICA
BERMUDA

Artist, Joseph Wilhelm painted the smart-looking *African Enterprise* departing from Cape Town. (Author's Collection)

Glen Line passenger-cargo ships could carry up to eighteen passengers. (Author's Collection)

Very popular with British passengers escaping the dreary, cold winters, the Fyffes Line ran sailings with the combo ships *Camito* and *Golfito*. (Author's Collection)

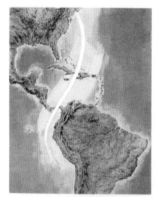

Far left: Innovation: The Grace Line Santa Maria-class ships were designed in the early 1960s to carry general cargo as well as some containers. (Andrew Kilk Collection)

Left: The joint Hamburg America Line–North German Lloyd service between Europe and the Far East was noted for its high standard of accommodation as well as service. (Andrew Kilk Collection)

DELTA LINE CRUISES TO SOUTH AMERICA

SANTA MERCEDES · SANTA MARIANA · SANTA MARIA · SANTA MAGDALENA

The attractive lounge of the eighty-six-bed *Frankfurt*. (Andrew Kilk Collection)

The bar aboard the *Hamburg*. (Andrew Kilk Collection)

Later used by the Delta Line, the Santa Maria-class ships were among the last combo liners under the US flag. (Andrew Kilk Collection)

Left: Holland–America Line passenger service included combo ships serving the North American west coast. (Author's Collection)

Below: A converted Victory ship, the Yugoslav-flag *Hrvatska* is seen berthed at Port Newark, New Jersey, within New York Harbor, in a photo from the early 1960s. (Port Authority of New York & New Jersey)

Above: The 134-passenger *Westerdam* is seen in the lower-centre position of Pier 40 at New York in a photo dated 1963. The *Statendam* is on the left; the *Rotterdam* at the top; and the freighter *Kinderdyk* on the right. (Holland–America Line)

Clockwise from below: Relaxation at sea: The inviting pool aboard the French *Cambodge*. (Messageries Maritimes); The former *Americana* seen at Lisbon in her final days as the tramp freighter *Golden Trade*. (Luis Miguel Correia); A painting of Ivaran Lines' passenger-container ship *Americana*. (Ivaran Lines)

LES MESSAGERIES MARITIMES ONT 120 ANS

Above: Messageries Maritimes offered diverse passenger ship services until the late 1960s. (Messageries Maritimes)

Right: The first-class smoking room aboard the *Laos*. (Messageries Maritimes).

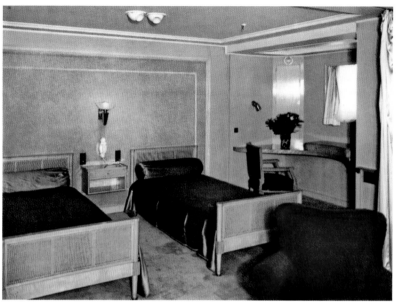

The bedroom of a first-class suite aboard the *Cambodge*. (Messageries Maritimes)

A fine painting of the *Viet-Nam*. (Author's Collection)

MESSAGERIES MARITIMES

"PASTEUR"

MODERNE AMBASSADEUR DE LA TRADITION FRANÇAISE
Modern ambassador of French tradition

Right: The last Messageries Maritimes passenger-cargo liner, the *Pasteur*, was commissioned in 1966. (Messageries Maritimes)

Left: The handsome-looking *Monte Ulia* of Spain's Aznar Line. (Author's Collection)

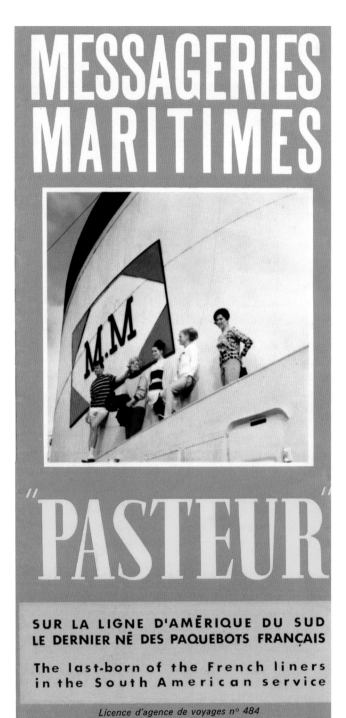

The Aznar ships used on the winter UK–Canaries run were known as 'friendly ships'. (Andrew Kilk Collection)

The *Pasteur* was also the last traditional passenger-cargo liner built for Europe–South America service. (Messageries Maritimes)

Come to Britain

TRAVEL BY

THE NEW ZEALAND SHIPPING COMPANY

RANGITOTO

RANGITANE

THE NEW ZEALAND SHIPPING COMPANY

Far left: New Zealand Shipping Company especially promoted return voyages to the UK. (Author's Collection)

Left: The 21,000-ton *Rangitane* and *Rangitoto* were the largest of the New Zealand Shipping Company's passenger-cargo liners. (Author's Collection)

The cover of a foldout deck plan of the *Ruahine*, built in 1951. (Author's Collection)

The Dutch-flag Oranje Line offered a unique passenger service between northern Europe, the St Lawrence Seaway and the Great Lakes. (Author's Collection)

A fine depiction of the *Remuera*, the former Cunard *Parthia*. (Author's Collection)

Far left: In her later years, Oranje's *Prinses Margriet* sailed as the *Enna G.* for the Nauru Pacific Line. (Andrew Kilk Collection)

Left: Chinese style: The passenger ship fleet of Orient Overseas Lines in the early 1970s. (Orient Overseas Line)

Golden Gate: The *Oriental Rio* at San Francisco. (Orient Overseas Line)

A cabin plan of Japan's *Brazil Maru*, built in 1954. (Andrew Kilk Collection)

A brochure cover for the three splendid Panama Line passenger ships commissioned in 1939. (Author's Collection)

Bound for Rio: The three combo ships of the Rotterdam–South America Line. (Author's Collection)

Holland's Royal Interocean Lines ran extensive passenger services until the late 1960s. (Author's Collection)

Na esteira do mundo

África do Sul, Mauritius, Malásia, Singapura, Hongkong, Japão... Argentina e Uruguai...

nas modernas motonaus da

ROYAL INTEROCEAN LINES

Banana boats to the sunny Caribbean: A poster depicting the white ships of the United Fruit Company. (Author's Collection)

The three sisters, *Boissevain*, *Ruys* and *Tegelberg*, were the largest passenger ships in the Royal Interocean fleet. (Author's Collection)

Yugoslavian style: The 475ft-long *Srbija* had been a German freighter, but was rebuilt to carry forty-four passengers in two classes. (Michael D.J. Lennon)

JUGOLINIJA

HRVATSKA AND *SRBIJA*

Headquartered in Rijeka, Jugolinija ran a combo service between the Mediterranean and New York as well as other US east coast ports. Their 7,904-ton *Hrvatska* was a former American Victory ship redesigned for sixty passengers and the 6,600-ton *Srbija*, an intended German freighter, carried up to forty-four passengers. These ships remained in service until the mid 1960s, when they were replaced by four new combo sister ships.

A former US-built Victory ship, the 7,904-ton *Hrvatska* was refitted to carry sixty one-class passengers in Mediterranean–New York service. (James McNamara Collection)

VISEVICA, KLEK, TUHOBIC AND *ZVIR*

Built in Yugoslavia in 1964–65, this quartet had accommodations for fifty passengers, with twenty in first class and thirty in tourist. They too were used in Mediterranean–US east coast service, but by 1980 were no longer profitable nor efficient. They were sold to Egyptian owners and renamed *Abu Hosna*, *Abu Alia*, *Abu Rashid* and *Abu Yossuf I*. The intention was to continue a Mediterranean–US service, but this soon failed and the four ships were sold off and later scrapped.

KHEDIVIAL MAIL LINE

KHEDIVE ISMAIL/CLEOPATRA AND *MOHAMMED ALI EL-KEBIR*

Built during the war, American-flag Victory ships were seen as ideal for conversion to passenger ships and often passenger-cargo combinations. The Egyptians transformed two of them, fitting in seventy-five passengers each. The 8,200grt *Khedive Ismail* (later renamed *Cleopatra*) and *Mohammed Ali El-Kebir* were used in regular service between New York, other US ports and the Mediterranean and Egypt, and later in an extended service to Pakistan and India.

MESSAGERIES MARITIMES

CAMBODGE, LAOS AND *VIET-NAM*

France had, until the late 1960s, maintained a sizeable fleet of passenger ships on eastern runs to the Middle East, east Africa and to the Far East, which included the vital link to colonial outposts in French Indo-China. To replace ageing, pre-war passenger ships such as the *Athos II*, *Felix Roussel*, *Champollion* and *La Marseillaise*, Messageries Maritimes built no fewer than nine combination passenger-cargo ships in the early 1950s. The largest, best decorated and last of these ships were built for the Far Eastern route. Built between 1952 and 1954, they were three very handsome ships, the 13,200grt sisters *Cambodge*, *Laos* and *Viet-Nam*. With five holds for cargo, they had accommodations for 347 total passengers (117 in first class, 110 in tourist class and 120 in third class). They ran a monthly rotation from Marseilles, sailing outbound to Port Said, Suez, Aden, Djibouti, Bombay, Colombo, Singapore, Saigon, Manila, Hong Kong, Kobe and Yokohama.

Passenger ship appraiser C.M. Squarey sailed aboard the brand-new *Viet-Nam* in the summer of 1954 and opined that, 'Her interior decoration gets right away from the old, heavy, dark Messageries Maritimes decor. Instead, it portrays so well all that is best, without going to extremes, in modern French decoration.'

Another converted Victory ship, Egypt's seventy-five-passenger *Cleopatra* is seen during the closure of the Suez Canal at a call at Cape Town. (James McNamara Collection)

French style: Among the finest combo liners of the 1950s, the *Cambodge* and her two sisters were very popular on the Marseilles–Far East run for Messageries Maritimes. (Messageries Maritimes)

The *Pacifique* and *Laos* were less fortunate, however. Both met with a fate quite well known to French and former French passenger ships: fire. They were sold in 1970 to the Abeto Line, a Panamanian firm with strong interests in the Muslim pilgrim trades as well as Far Eastern passenger services. The *Pacifique*, renamed *Princess Abeto*, was rebuilt at Hong Kong for as many as 1,612 passengers and the *Laos* was renamed *Empress Abeto* carrying up to 1,696 passengers. Their days were numbered, however.

The *Princess Abeto* (ex-*Viet-Nam*, ex-*Pacifique*), leased to the Fir Line and renamed *Malaysia Baru* and then *Malaysia Kita*, burned out while at a Singapore shipyard on 12 May 1974. Abandoned and left to sink, she was a declared a complete loss and her charred remains were towed to Taiwan two years later and broken up at Kaohsiung. The *Empress Abeto* (ex-*Laos*) was also chartered to the Fir Line, becoming the *Malaysia Raya*. She burned out at Port Klang and her remains were delivered to Kaohsiung scrappers in the summer of 1977.

CALEDONIEN AND TAHITIEN

The operations of these three ships, known as the 'Three Musketeers', went unchanged until 1967. When the Suez Canal was temporarily closed, the three were routed via South Africa, stopping at Cape Town and Durban, which in due course cut into their profits. Shortly afterward and prompted by political turmoil in South-east Asia, the *Viet-Nam* was renamed *Pacifique* (in September 1967). She was then used briefly on a new around-the-world service, sailing outward from Marseilles to the Caribbean, the Panama Canal and then homeward via South Africa. She was soon switched, however, to the Marseilles–Madagascar run. Meanwhile, the *Cambodge* and *Laos* were to be shifted to the Marseilles–South Pacific–Australia run, replacing two other company combination ships, the *Caledonien* and *Tahitien* (qv). Operational costs soared as passenger loads dropped drastically, however. The *Cambodge* and *Laos* were never moved to a different service and were prematurely retired in late 1969. The *Pacifique* followed a year later.

Laid up for a time at Marseilles, the 532ft-long *Cambodge* was sold in 1969 to the Sun Line, a Greek cruise operator. She was partially gutted, then rebuilt and reappeared as the all-first-class, 765-passenger cruise ship *Stella Solaris*. Spending most of her year in Aegean and eastern Mediterranean waters, she was later used for winter cruising in the Caribbean and South America. She was finally scrapped, after nearly fifty years of service, in 2003.

Another of the numerous Messageries Maritimes passenger services was the long-haul run from Marseilles out to the South Pacific. The actual itinerary read: Algiers, Martinique, Guadeloupe, Panama Canal, French Polynesia, New Hebrides, New Caledonia and Sydney. The last ships used on this run were also combination passenger-cargo liners, the *Caledonien* and *Tahitien* – the former completed in September 1952, the latter in May 1953. At 12,700 tons, they had three-class accommodations, with seventy in first class, eight-four in tourist class and 208 in third class.

They carried many government passengers and their families, supplies and the all-important mail to far-off outposts. Having sailed for almost twenty years, just before they were to be retired the 549ft-long *Tahitien* suffered an engine room fire while in the Pacific, on 2 May 1969. Disabled, she had to be towed to Panama and temporarily repaired before returning to Marseilles for four months in late August. Following major repairs, she resumed sailing in late May, but for less than two years. In 1971, the *Caledonien* was laid up and then sold to Greek buyers, the Efthymiadis Lines, and renamed *Nisos Kypros* and shortly afterwards *Island of Cyprus*. She was used mostly on the Piraeus–Heraklion (Cyprus) ferry run until sold to ship breakers in 1975. After being sold to other Greek owners known as Aphrodite Cruises, the *Tahitien* was extensively rebuilt as the cruise ship *Atalante*. She sailed mostly in the eastern Mediterranean cruise service until scrapped in 2005.

The 492ft-long *Jean Laborde* seen at Durban. (Alex Duncan)

FERDINAND DE LESSEPS, *JEAN LABORDE*, *LA BOURDONNAIS* AND *PIERRE LOTI*

This quartet of 10,900-tonners were in fact the smallest of this Messageries Maritimes group. They were designed especially for the East African trade to Mauritius. The 492ft-long *La Bourdonnais* was the first of the class, being launched at Lorient in July 1951. The *Ferdinand De Lesseps* followed, then the *Pierre Loti* and finally, in July 1953, the *Jean Laborde*.

The four ships had five cargo holds, around a third of which capacity was for refrigerated items, and three-class passenger quarters: 88 in first class, 112 in second class and 299 in third class (later reduced to forty berths). First class was comprised of several suites and large staterooms, all of them with private bathrooms as well as several public rooms, a small restaurant, sun deck and outdoor pool. Tourist class was slightly less spacious and comfortable, and had only three- and four-berth cabins (without private facilities). Third class, used primarily for troops, police and workers, was quite basic and offered four-berth rooms and small dormitories.

These four ships were retired and sold to Greek buyers in the late 1960s. Joining the Efthymiadis Lines, *La Bourdonnais* became the Aegean-routed *Knossos*. She had an engine room fire on 3 May 1973, however, and was towed to port and then laid up until handed over to Spanish ship breakers in 1976. The *Ferdinand des Lesseps* became the *Delphi* for Efthymiadis until sold, in 1977, to other Greek owners, becoming *La Perla* and then *La Palma*. After some fifty years of service, she was scrapped in 2003. The *Pierre Loti* became the *Olimpia*, *Patra*, *Chrysouvalandou II* and finally *Eros* before being demolished in 1986. Finally, the *Jean Laborde* became the *Mykinai*, *Ancona*, *Brindisi Express* and *Eastern Princess* until, in the late 1970s, being rebuilt as the 800-berth cruise ship *Oceanos*. She made headlines when, after flooding, she sank off the South African coast on 4 August 1991. Fortunately, all passengers and crew were saved.

PASTEUR

This 17,986grt ship was the last combo liner built for Messageries Maritimes. Completed in 1966 and fitted with fine quarters for 429 passengers (163 in first class and 266 in tourist class), she was intended to be the *Australien* for the Marseilles–South Pacific–Australia service, but was completed instead as the *Pasteur* for the North Europe–east coast of South America trade. Sold in 1972 to the Shipping Corporation of India and renamed *Chidambaram* (carrying 154 cabin and 1,526 deck passengers), the 571ft ship was used in India–Singapore service. Sadly, however, she was destroyed by fire in the Bay of Bengal in February 1985. Fifty lives were lost and the burnt-out hull was later towed to Bombay and scrapped.

NAVIERA AZNAR

MONTE UDALA, MONTE URBASA, MONTE ULIA, MONTE UMBE, MONTE URQUIOLA, MONTE ARUCAS AND *MONTE ANAGA*

Based in Bilbao, Naviera Aznar ran a good-sized fleet of combo liners in the 1950s and '60s, mostly between the UK and the Canary Islands, and between Spain, other Mediterranean ports and the east coast of South America. This company was very popular in UK travel circles with their winter cruise-like voyages to Las Palmas and Tenerife and, in London, were familiar sights at the New Fresh Wharves in the Pool of London.

NEW ZEALAND SHIPPING CO.

RANGITANE, RANGITOTO AND *RUAHINE*

With London-based New Zealand Shipping Company (NZSCO), John Jones served as a steward on the 21,000-ton *Rangitoto*, which carried over 400 passengers in all-one-class quarters: 'NZ Shipping, as it was called, was said to be a cut above Shaw Savill,' he remembered, adding, 'The NZSCO ships were faster and more comfortable'.

Sailing between London via Curaçao and Panama to Auckland and Wellington (and other New Zealand ports), the 21,800grt sisters *Rangitane* and *Rangitoto*, carrying up to 416 passengers each, dated from 1949 and were the largest combo liners in the fleet. The 17,800grt *Ruahine* was a modified, slightly smaller version, carrying 267 passengers. She dated from 1951. These ships were sold off in the late 1960s to the Orient Overseas Line (qv).

Special occasion: One of the largest ships ever to berth in the Pool of London, the 10,000grt *Monte Ulia* passes under Tower Bridge. The ship called on 31 May 1953, bringing pre-Coronation visitors to London. (Cronican-Arroyo Collection)

Alternate sailings: Normally carrying up to seventy-four passengers on the Spain–Canaries run, the 7,723grt *Monte Urquiola* is seen during a detour. Here she is shown loading scrap metal at Port Newark, New Jersey. The photograph is dated September 1959 and the scrap metals are being sent to Spain for recycling. (Gillespie-Faber Collection)

HOMEWARD SAILINGS—1965

		Sails N.Z.		Due Tahiti		Due Panama		Due Kingston		Due Port Everglades		Due Bermuda		Due U.K.	
RANGITOTO	..	Jan.	9	Jan.	15	Jan.	28	Jan.	31	Feb.	2	Feb.	6	Feb.	15
RANGITANE	..	Feb.	27	Mar.	5	Mar	18	Mar	21	Mar	23	Mar.	27	Apr	5
RUAHINE		Mar	27	Apr	1	Apr	13	Apr	16	Apr.	18	Apr	22	Apr	30
RANGITOTO		May	19	May	25	June	7	June	10	June	12	June	16	June	25
RANGITANE	..	June	30	July	6	July	19	July	22	July	24	July	28	Aug.	6
*RUAHINE		July	31	Aug.	5	Aug.	17	Aug.	20	Aug.	22	Aug.	26	Sept.	3
*RANGITOTO		Oct.	6	Oct.	12	Oct.	25	Oct.	28	Oct.	30	Nov	3	Nov	12
*RANGITANE		Nov	6	Nov	12	Nov	25	Nov	28	Nov	30	Dec.	4	Dec.	13
										1966		1966		1966	
*RUAHINE	..	Dec.	11	Dec.	16	Dec.	28	Dec.	31	Jan.	2	Jan.	6	Jan.	14

*Off Season Sailings for which reduced rates apply

A sailing schedule from 1965. (Andrew Kilk Collection)

Above: The 21,867grt *Rangitane* and *Rangitoto* were among the largest combination passenger-cargo liners of their time. Carrying up to 416 passengers each, they were commissioned in 1949 for UK–New Zealand service. (New Zealand Shipping Co.)

Left: Slightly smaller and carrying fewer passengers (267 in all), the *Ruahine* was added in 1951. (New Zealand Shipping Co.)

Formerly Cunard's *Parthia*, the *Remuera* was modified in 1961–62 to suit New Zealand Shipping Company's preferences. (New Zealand Shipping Co.)

The same ship, but now seen as the *Aramac* for the Eastern & Australian Line. (Eastern & Australian Line)

ORANJE LINE

PRINS WILLEM VAN ORANJE, PRINSES IRENE AND *PRINSES MARGRIET*

Holland's Oranje Line began running freighter service, with twelve passengers or less, to eastern Canada in the late 1930s. It was not until the early 1950s, however, that, while creating their largest ship yet, they increased their passenger ship presence. When the 7,300grt *Prins Willem van Oranje* was commissioned in the late summer of 1953, she had sixty first-class berths. She traded between Rotterdam, Southampton and Montreal (to Halifax and St John, New Brunswick in winter). Then, once the St Lawrence Seaway opened in 1959, the company decided to extend its services into the Great Lakes. It would be a unique, and potentially prosperous, venture.

In the late 1950s, the company strengthened its overall position. They merged with the Norwegian-flag Fjell Line and thereafter were retitled as the Fjell-Oranje Line. (The passenger division was always referred to as the Oranje Line, however.) Furthermore, the Oranje Line was sold to a Dutch partnership that included the Holland–America Line. Finally, the company decided to extend its passenger services to the Great Lakes and add two, well-appointed combination passenger-cargo liners, the near sisters *Prinses Irene* and *Prinses Margriet*.

The 8,526grt *Prinses Irene*, which was named for Princess Irene, a daughter of Queen Juliana of the Netherlands, entered service in April 1959. The 456ft-long ship participated in the official opening of the St Lawrence Seaway and was thereafter able to proceed to Chicago, Toronto and other Great Lakes ports. It was in fact an Oranje Line freighter, the *Prins Willem Oranje Frederik* that became the very first overseas commercial vessel to use the new seaway. The *Prinses Margriet* – also named for a daughter of Queen Juliana – was commissioned two years later, in July 1961. Both ships received high praise, having been well designed and decorated, with all the passenger cabins fitted with private facilities.

The three ships – the *Prins Willem van Oranje*, *Prinses Irene* and *Prinses Margriet* – maintained a transatlantic service out of Rotterdam and Southampton. Mini cruises were also offered during the interport segments between Chicago and Montreal. In winter, the ships went to Halifax and St John (the *Prinses Irene* did make several trips to the Gulf of Mexico, with turnarounds at Vera Cruz and Tampico). However, the Oranje passenger service was not wildly successful and was, in fact, quite disappointing. Even the company's cargo trade was not a sufficient alternative. In 1962, as

The 459ft-long *Prinses Margriet* passes through the St Lawrence Seaway on one of her extended voyages to the North American Great Lakes. (Halifax Maritime Museum)

something of a first step, the *Prins Willem van Oranje* was reduced to a twelve-passenger freighter. Shortly thereafter, in the spring of 1963, the still new *Prinses Margriet* was chartered to the Holland–America Line for their Rotterdam–New York direct service, replacing the aged *Noordam* and paired with another combo liner, the *Westerdam*. The *Prinses Irene* closed out Oranje passenger service at the end of the summer season of 1963. She was then chartered to Cunard for a year as a cargo ship, mostly for the so-called 'whiskey run' between Glasgow and New York.

Busy afternoon: In this 1963 view, the *Prinses Margriet* is berthed on the outer end of Pier 40, New York. The *Rotterdam* is just arriving on the left and the Norwegian *Stavangerfjord* is visible between the two ships. (Moran Towing & Transportation Co.)

M.S. PRINSES MARGRIET

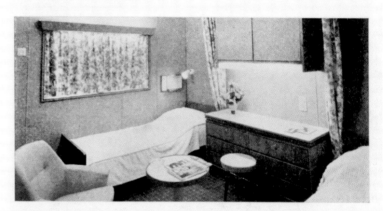

HUT/CABIN M.S. PRINSES MARGRIET

LOUNGE M.S. PRINS WILLEM VAN ORANJE

Comfort at sea: Accommodations aboard the short-lived Oranje Line passenger-cargo ships. (Andrew Kilk Collection)

The *Margriet* was finally bought outright by Holland–America in December 1964. At the same time, with her Cunard charter concluded, the *Irene* was sold to the Dutch Verolme Shipyard and then shortly thereafter resold to Indonesia's Djakarta Lloyd. She was extensively rebuilt with some 900 berths, mostly for the Muslim pilgrim trade across the Indian Ocean to Jeddah. Renamed *Tjut Njak Dhien*, she was transferred in 1979 to the Indonesian navy and used as the troop transport *Tanjung Oisina*. She was scrapped in 2013.

The last Oranje passenger ship (although reduced to a freighter), the *Prins Willem van Oranje* left the fleet in February 1965. She was sold to the East German government and became the *Ferdinand Freiligrath*. A decade or so later, in the mid 1970s, she passed to Panamanian-flag owners for general tramping purposes and in succession became *Freijo*, *Universal Honolulu* and finally *August 8th*. Laid up at Singapore in October 1977, she was scrapped two years later on Taiwan.

The *Prinses Margriet* finished her Holland–America north Atlantic service in late 1967 and then went to another Dutch firm, the Royal Netherlands Steamship Company, for a series of twelve-day cruises from New York to the Caribbean. It was a very late-day use of a combination ship in the otherwise highly competitive American cruise industry. While Holland–America continued as her passenger agents, her operations were again quite unprofitable. She was sold in 1970 to the government of the Republic of Nauru, the phosphate-rich island in the western Pacific. Renamed *Enna G*, she ran six-week passenger-cargo cruises for the Nauru-Pacific Line out of San Francisco to Honolulu, Majuro, Ponape, Truk and Saipan. In the early part of 1984 she was laid up and said to be 'mechanically exhausted'. She was broken up in Thailand in 1990.

As for the Oranje Line itself, long after giving up passenger service, its operations slumped even further. The company ceased trading altogether at the end of 1969.

ORIENT OVERSEAS LINE

ORIENTAL JADE AND *ORIENTAL PEARL*

Beginning in the mid 1960s, Hong Kong-based shipping tycoon C.Y. Tung began to add combo ships to his expanding freighter fleet. The ships he chose were the former *Excalibur* and *Exeter*, of American Export Lines. Added in 1964, these 124-passenger ships were used in a transpacific service from San Francisco to Yokohama, Kobe, Pusan, Inchon, Keelung, Kaohsiung and Hong Kong, and then return. The round trip took approximately fifty-six days. These ships endured for almost a decade until, with soaring fuel oil costs, they were retired and scrapped in Taiwan in 1974.

ORIENTAL CARNAVAL, ORIENTAL ESMERALDA, ORIENTAL RIO, ORIENTAL AMIGA AND *ORIENTAL FANTASIA*

By 1968–69, Tung and his Orient Overseas division wanted to expand into the around-the-world passenger service using five combo ships. The 19,500grt *Oriental Carnaval* and *Oriental Esmeralda* – the former *Rangitoto* and *Rangitane* (built in 1948–49) of New Zealand Shipping Company – were refitted to carry 300 all first-class passengers. They flew the Liberian colours and set off on four-month world voyages, from Los Angeles to Acapulco, the Panama Canal, Port Everglades, Rio de Janeiro, Santos, Buenos Aires, Cape Town, Durban, Lourenço Marques, Singapore, Hong Kong, Kaohsiung, Keelung, Kobe, Yokohama, Vancouver and return to Los Angeles. Later used in a shorter Central American service, they were laid up in 1973–74 and then scrapped two years later.

The 267-passenger *Oriental Rio*, the former *Ruahine* (1951), also from New Zealand Shipping, joined this world service in 1968 until laid up in 1973 and then scrapped a year later.

With a rebuilt upper bow, the *Oriental Jade* (the former *Excalibur* of American Export) is seen berthed at San Francisco. (Alex Duncan)

Bon voyage: The *Oriental Esmeralda* (the one-time *Rangitane* of Britain's New Zealand Shipping Company) is outbound from San Francisco on another around-the-world voyage. She is seen passing under the Bay Bridge. (Luis Miguel Correia Collection)

Finally, to complete the around-the-world group and providing almost monthly sailings, Tung added the *Oriental Amiga* and *Oriental Fantasia*, both sixty-passenger combo ships that had once been the *Diemerdyk* (1950) and *Dinteldyk* (1957) of Holland–America. Later used in transpacific service, they were victims of the mass shift to containerisation by the mid 1970s. Both ships, used as partial container ships in their final years, sailed on until sold to Taiwanese scrappers in 1979.

Dressed in flags: Inbound on her maiden arrival, the *Oriental Rio*, the former *Ruahine*, arrives at San Francisco. (Orient Overseas Line)

Redecorating: The *Oriental Ruler* and her five sisters, all former Germans, were given a more Asian tone and style following their takeover by Orient Overseas Line. (Alex Duncan)

ORIENTAL HERO, ORIENTAL INVENTOR, ORIENTAL WARRIOR, ORIENTAL LADY, ORIENTAL MUSICIAN AND *ORIENTAL RULER*

These six West German combo liners, previously the *Frankfurt, Hamburg, Hannover, Bayernstein, Hessenstein* and *Schwabenstein*, were acquired in 1966–67 and renamed. Still carrying up to eighty-six passengers each, they were assigned to 120-day round-trip voyages from New York, Baltimore, Charleston, New Orleans, Houston, Galveston and then a transit through the Panama Canal before calling at Los Angeles, and then continuing across the Pacific to Yokohama, Nagoya, Kobe, Pusan, Yosu and/or Inchon, Keelung, Kaohsiung and Hong Kong. Passenger fares were a great bargain, beginning at as little as $14 a day. Passenger operations continued in full force until 1973, when dramatically increased fuel oil prices curtailed many of Tung's passenger-carrying services. By 1976, all six of these former German ships were downgraded and used in the tramp trades. The *Oriental Warrior* (ex-*Hamburg*) was lost by fire off the coast of Florida in 1972 and the other five were subsequently broken up at either Hong Kong or Kaohsiung, Taiwan in 1978–79.

OSAKA SHOSEN KAISHA

BRAZIL MARU, ARGENTINA MARU, AFRICA MARU, AMERICA MARU AND *SANTOS MARU*

Following the Second World War, migration by sea to a multitude of destinations was popular. Tens of thousands sought new lives elsewhere, new homes, new jobs and new freedom. Europeans headed to North America, to the United States and Canada, as well as the British going to Australia, the Italians to Brazil and Argentina, the Portuguese to Africa and the Spanish to Venezuela. There was also a big flow of Japanese to the east coast of South America, particularly to Brazil. Special passenger ships, run by the OSK Line (Osaka Shosen Kaisha) and later merged as the Mitsui-OSK Line, were used for some twenty years, beginning in the early 1950s.

Japanese passenger ship service to South America resumed in 1952. According to Hisashi Noma, Japan's pre-eminent maritime historian:

It was called the 'Outward Project' and was purposely created for Japanese immigrants going to Brazil and also to Uruguay, Paraguay and Argentina. Jobs were very scarce in Japan and so the flow of passengers resumed quickly. OSK had a passenger liner run to South America until 1940. Myself, I attended

Fleet mates: The *Argentina Maru* is on the outer side and the *Brazil Maru* is behind in this rare meeting of the two ships at Yokohama. (Hisashi Noma Collection)

actually owned some of the largest farms in Brazil. It was ideal for the 1950s. There was no resistance in getting thousands to go. These OSK liners were quite full – and quite profitable. Japanese migrants also used third class on the Dutch-flag Royal Interocean liners, the *Ruys*, *Tegelberg*, *Boissevain* and *Tjitjalengka*, but which sailed to South America via Southeast Asia, the Indian Ocean and South Africa.

Gradually, however, this Japanese migrant trade began to decline in the 1960s. Sea travel itself was to undergo drastic changes as well, especially as airlines became fierce, almost ferocious competitors. As Hisashi Noma describes:

The OSK Line wanted to maintain this service because passenger ships had priority berthing in South American ports ... Otherwise, there might be twenty-, thirty-, even forty-day waits for a berth, especially in ports such as La Guaira in Venezuela. The 'fixed' schedule was very important and so

the reception for the post-war inaugural voyage of the *Santos Maru* in the winter of 1952.

The 8,500grt *Santos Maru* had been a freighter, but then was especially refitted for the migrant trade. She had twelve berths in freighter-style first class, fifty in 'special' third class and then 558 in dormitory-style third class. Quite soon, two other ships, the *Africa Maru* and *America Maru*, joined her. They had been built initially for the Japan–Panama Canal–New York cargo run. In 1954, they were joined by Japan's first newly built post-war passenger ship, the 10,100grt *Brazil Maru*. She could carry twelve in cabin class and 970 third-class passengers. The demand for berths increased steadily. The slightly larger *Argentina Maru* was added four years later. Generally, these two ships were updated copies of two 1939-built ships, the earlier *Argentina Maru* and *Brazil Maru*.

According to Hisashi Noma, 'There were almost no homeward passengers on this South American service':

The bunks for third class were in the cargo holds and were collapsible. On the return trips, these were dismantled and the space used for freight – cottons and wools mostly. Migrant figures to South America from Japan rose to their highest level in 1958–59. Immigration in the 1920s and '30s had been strong and South America had been neutral during the war. Already, there was a sizeable Japanese population there. Mostly, they were in farming and some Japanese

The converted freighter *Africa Maru* is outbound at Yokohama with passengers, mostly migrants headed for South America. (Hisashi Noma Collection)

Conversion: Restyled for cruising, the former *Argentina Maru* sailed as the *Nippon Maru* until 1977. (MOPASS)

Transit: The good-looking *Cristobal* passing through the Panama Canal. (James McNamara Collection)

the passenger spaces were retained even though they became less and less profitable. When the Mitsui Line merged with OSK in 1964, they decided to resume actual trans-Pacific passenger service. They refitted the *Brazil Maru* and *Argentina Maru*, and made third class into more comfortable economy class. On-board standards improved. Now, there was a greater promotion for Japan–Hawaii and Japan–California services.

While the *Santos Maru*, *Africa Maru* and *America Maru* were later reduced to freighter status and finally sold off for general tramping, the *Brazil Maru* was retired and promptly became a museum ship at Toba, Japan in 1973 (and in China from 1996) while the *Argentina Maru* sailed as the cruise ship *Nippon Maru* for three years beginning in 1973 and was then demolished in Taiwan.

PANAMA LINE

ANCON, CRISTOBAL AND *PANAMA*

Three of the very finest examples of combo design, this art deco trio was created in 1939 purposely for government-related service between New York and the Panama Canal Zone. Carrying up to 216 passengers each, the 10,000grt *Panama* went on to become the *President Hoover* in 1957 (and later the *Regina* and *Regina Prima*). The *Ancon* later sailed as the training ship *State of Maine*, while the *Cristobal* continued under her original name until the end of her days in 1981.

P&O LINES

CHITRAL AND *CATHAY*

Soon after P&O and the Orient Line merged their services, becoming P&O-Orient Lines, there were changes made within the passenger fleet. The aged *Corfu*, *Carthage* and *Canton*, all dating from the 1930s, were retired from UK–Far East run. While P&O was not interested in building replacements, they were very fortunate to find two splendid passenger-cargo liners, the *Jadotville* and *Baudouinville*, suddenly available for sale. Built in 1956–57, their owners, the Compagnie Maritime Belge, saw a sudden downturn in requirements on the African run following the political independence of the Belgian Congo. P&O bought both ships for £3 million. Little was needed other than name changes, whereby the *Jadotville* became the *Chitral* and entered her new service in March 1961 and the *Baudouinville* changed to *Cathay* and started Far East sailings a month later, in April. They were very successful ships, being routed on seventy-day round trips stopping at London, Rotterdam, Southampton, Port Said, Aden, Colombo, Penang, Port Swettenham, Singapore, Hong Kong, Kobe and Yokohama. On the return trips, these 240-passenger ships made a stop at Naples as well.

By the late 1960s, however, the cargo that filled their six holds began to go in a new generation of faster, more efficient container ships. The economics of operating combo ships was changing rapidly. There was talk of rebuilding them as full passenger ships, with greater capacities, but such ideas never materialised.

The *Cathay* was withdrawn in late 1969 and transferred over to a P&O affiliate, the Melbourne-based Eastern & Australian Steamship Company. She retained her name, but hereafter had Australian officers and a Chinese crew. She was now routed on a triangular service from Melbourne, Sydney and Brisbane north to Manila, Hong Kong, Yokkaichi, Nagoya, Kobe, Yokohama and then homeward via Guam.

The *Chitral* proved, by 1970, to be the very last passenger ship on P&O's old Far East run. It was rumoured she would become a hotel ship moored in the Indian Ocean or be refitted and downgraded as a twelve-passenger

The *Chitral* visiting Valletta harbour on Malta in this view dating from April 1966. (P&O)

freighter. Instead, P&O made the decision to place the ship on April–October cruises in the Mediterranean out of Genoa. This was a mistake, however, as there were no easy air connections from the UK. A ship carrying 240 passengers with six empty cargo holds was hardly economic. By late 1970, she too joined Eastern & Australian and was soon sailing on the Australia–Far East route.

The *Cathay* and *Chitral* were popular with passengers, but again out of step in the container age. They were retired by December 1975. The *Cathay* was fortunate and found a buyer in the Macao-based Nan Yang Shipping Company for use as a merchant marine training ship. She soon passed to the China Ocean Shipping Company, however, and was renamed *Shanghai* for short-sea service between Shanghai and Hong Kong. She was finally broken up in 1996. The *Chitral* was less fortunate, however, and was quickly sold to Taiwanese scrappers in 1976.

ROTTERDAM–SOUTH AMERICA LINE

ALDABI, ALHENA AND ALNATI

These 7,300-ton ships, carrying up to fifty passengers each, ran regular service between northern Europe and ports along the east coast of South America.

ROYAL INTEROCEAN LINES

STRAAT BANKA AND TJINEGARA

Although Dutch, the ships of the Royal Interocean Lines (RIL) rarely touched in at home waters, but instead ran in one of the world's most extensive passenger and freight networks, that which connected the east coast of South America with south and east Africa, then the Middle East, the Far East and across to Australia. Their passenger fleet in the 1950s and '60s consisted of a number of two- and three-class passenger ships carrying several hundred travellers each. The sisters *Straat Banka* and *Tjinegara* were the exceptions.

Built at Rotterdam in 1951, these ships were designed as high-standard passenger-cargo ships carrying no more than fifty passengers each. The 472ft-long *Straat Banka* was used on a separate RIL passenger service, connecting India and Australia, and assisted by freighters only. Alternately,

the *Tjinegara* worked the long-haul service between the three continents with the company passenger ships.

Dr David Kirkman served aboard the 9,000grt *Straat Banka* as ship's doctor in the 1960s. He recalled how the the *Straat Banka* worked 'what we called the "Indian run" between Bombay, Cochin, Colombo, Penang, Singapore, Jakarta, Brisbane, Sydney and Melbourne':

We'd take tallow and livestock to India, and then spices and tea in return to Australian ports. These ships, like all vessels run by Royal Interocean, had exceptional Dutch captains. So experienced and so precise, it was said that these men could simply look over the side and know where they were just

The *Straat Banka*, carrying up to fifty first-class passengers, arriving at Sydney. On her India–Australia sailings, she was assisted by two smaller freighters, carrying up to twelve passengers. (Richard Faber Collection)

m s „Straat Banka"

Outbound for South American ports, the forty-five-passenger *Aldabi* passes through the English Channel with the Dover cliffs in the background. (Gillespie-Faber Collection)

Pleasant quarters aboard the three Rotterdam-South America Line combo ships. (Andrew Kilk Collection)

by the colour and quality of the water. One old commander taught himself Chinese and Japanese while at sea and did so well that, in retirement, he became a professor of Asian languages at Sydney University. These captains raised their families in the east, but when their sons followed them to nautical colleges at Amsterdam and Rotterdam, Holland was a strange, very foreign country to them. Royal Interocean usually hired only Dutch officers, with a handful of Chinese pursers and Indonesians as the crew.

In the early 1970s, ships like the *Straat Banka* and the *Tjinegara* as well were facing the mandatory twenty-year refit prescribed by Dutch maritime law … Overcoming such an obstacle, Royal Interocean formed a 'flag of convenience' subsidiary, the Mercury Shipping Company of Hong Kong, but which was actually a one-room office with a typewriter. Like some other Company ships, the *Straat Banka* and *Tjinegara* changed hands as well as flags, becoming the *Mercury Lake* and *Mercury Bay* respectively. They were put straight into freight service, tramping about mostly carrying second-hand cars to Indonesia. Near the end, I met up with my old ship, the former *Straat Banka*, and was horrified to see automotive 'heaps' stored even in the former passenger lounge and restaurant. Both ships, by then in very poor, rundown condition, were broken-up for scrap in the late 1970s.

ROYAL NETHERLANDS STEAMSHIP CO.

ORANJE NASSAU AND *PRINS DER NEDERLANDEN*

These 7,200-ton sister ships belonged to Amsterdam-based Royal Netherlands Steamship Company. Built in 1957 for service to the Caribbean from northern Europe, they carried 116 first-class passengers as well as sixty-eight in economy quarters.

ORANJESTAD AND *WILLEMSTAD*

Built in 1938 and converted as passenger ships in 1950, for ninety-four first-class and sixty-two economy-class passengers, this 5,000-ton pair serviced colonial Suriname from northern Europe.

ROYAL ROTTERDAM LLOYD

MODJOKERTO, MATARAM, SLAMAT, BLITAR AND *LANGKOEAS*

While the larger 10,100-ton *Modjokerto* was a wartime standard-type freighter, she was like the others in carrying up to thirty-five passengers each. While all were mostly used on the North Europe–Middle & Far East runs, the other four could carry up to 1,400 deck passengers, mostly pilgrims, out to eastern waters.

The 7,200grt *Prins der Nederlanden* and her sister, the *Oranje Nassau*, were the largest units in the otherwise big Royal Netherlands fleet of the late 1950s. (Gillespie-Faber Collection)

Converted from cargo ships, the 5,000grt sisters *Oranjestad* and *Willemstad* (shown) were among the smallest combo ships of their time. (Alex Duncan)

Heavily loaded with Dutch-made goods, the *Modjokerto* plows to eastern ports. A 10,100-ton vessel completed in 1946, she was adapted to carry up to thirty-six passengers in eighteen double-berth cabins. (Royal Rotterdam Lloyd)

Large scale: The mighty, 15,896grt *Ceramic* was built to carry eighty-five all-first-class passengers, but is seen here in the late 1960s and near the end of her days when she was downgraded to freighter-only service. (Steffen Weirauch)

SHAW SAVILL LINE

ATHENIC, CORINTHIC, CERAMIC AND *GOTHIC*

Four of the biggest post-war combo liners, the 15–16,000-ton quartet of the *Athenic*, *Corinthic*, *Ceramic* and *Gothic*, were added to the Shaw Savill Line in 1947–48 for the UK–New Zealand trade. Designed to carry large quantities of frozen meat on homeward sailings, they had very comfortable quarters for up to eighty-five passengers each. The 561ft-long *Gothic* had an added distinction – she was used in 1953–54 as a temporary Royal Yacht carrying Queen Elizabeth II and the Duke of Edinburgh around the world. Eventually outmoded, these ships were sold for scrap in the late 1960s and early '70s.

SPLOSNA PLOVBA

BLED, BOVEC AND *BOHINJ*

Former Belgian freighters built during the Second World War, these 7,700-ton ships were used on the Atlantic run, sailing between Rijeka and New York. Each ship carried up to sixty passengers.

The *Gothic* being converted in 1951 at the Cammell Laird Shipyard at Birkenhead for duties as a Royal Yacht in 1952. She was to take King George VI, Queen Elizabeth and Princess Margaret on a Commonwealth Tour. The voyage was cancelled, however, due to the king's increasingly poor health, but was rescheduled for November 1953–May 1954 for Queen Elizabeth II and the Duke of Edinburgh. (Cronican-Arroyo Collection)

The *Bohinj*, seen arriving at Boston, and her two sisters could carry up to sixty passengers each on transatlantic voyages between the US east coast and the Mediterranean. (Michael D.J. Lennon)

UNITED FRUIT COMPANY

JAMAICA, QUIRIGUA, VERAGUA, TALAMANCA, ANTIGUA AND *CHIRIQUI*

In the early 1930s, this well-known firm, dubbed 'the Great White Fleet', built six mailboats with 100 passenger berths each for US–Caribbean and Central American services. There were plans to build slightly larger, better-appointed versions as late as 1945–46, but they never emerged. By the late 1940s, these six ships were divided in their operations: three sailed out of New Orleans, the other three from New York. By the mid 1950s, however, they were money losers, sailing as much as two-thirds empty. Later reduced to freighters, including some service with Elders & Fyffes and under the British flag, they were scrapped in the 1960s.

ZIM LINES

ISRAEL AND *ZION*

Two splendidly designed ships, this 9,900-ton pair, built out of a West German reparations account to Israel, carried up to 313 passengers in first- and tourist-class quarters. Completed in 1955–56, they sailed between Haifa, other Mediterranean ports and New York.

Mailboat to the tropics: A splendid aerial view of United Fruit's *Talamanca*. (Steamship Historical Society of America)

Israel's first newly built passenger ship, the 313-berth, West German-built *Israel* arrives in New York for the first time, in a view dated 27 October 1955. The 501ft-long ship berthed specially at Pier 88, the French Line terminal, for the gala occasion. Behind, from left to right, are the *United States*, *Conte Biancamano* and *Constitution*. (James McNamara Collection)

BIBLIOGRAPHY

Collard, Ian. *Blue Funnel Line: An Illustrated History*. Stroud, Gloucestershire: Amberley Publishing, 2010.

Dunn, Laurence. *Passenger Liners*. London: Adlard Coles Ltd, 1961 (2nd Edition, 1965).

Heine, Frank & Lose, Frank. *Great Passenger Ships of the World*. Hamburg, Germany: Koehlers Verlagsgesellschaft, 2010.

Kludas, Arnold. *Great Passenger Ships of the World: Vol. 4, 1936–50*. Cambridge: Patrick Stephens Ltd, 1977.

Kludas, Arnold. *Great Passenger Ships of the World: Vol. 5, 1951–76*. Cambridge: Patrick Stephens Ltd, 1977.

Mayes, William. *Cruise Ships* (Fourth Edition). Windsor, England: Overview Press Ltd, 2011.

Miller, William H. & Noble, Tim. *East of Suez: Liners to Australia in the 1950s & 1960s*. Stroud, Gloucestershire: Amberley Publishing, 2013.

Miller, William H. *Great American Passenger Ships*. Stroud, Gloucestershire: The History Press, 2012.

Miller, William H. *Greek Passenger Liners*. Stroud, Gloucestershire: Tempus Publishing Ltd, 2006.

Miller, William H. *Pictorial Encyclopaedia of Ocean Liners, 1860–1994*. Mineola, New York: Dover Publications Inc., 1995.

Miller, William H. *Under the Red Ensign: British Passenger Ships of the 1950s & 1960s*. Stroud, Gloucestershire: The History Press, 2009.

Ocean & Cruise News (1980–2014). Northport, New York: World Ocean & Cruise Liner Society.

Official Steamship Guide (1951–63). New York City: Transportation Guides Inc.